Timeshare Owner's Guide to
Winning the Timeshare Game

Timeshare Owner's Guide to

Winning the Timeshare Game

Winning the Timeshare Game

How to Master the Game and Make Your Timeshare Work for You

By Deanna Keahey

Timeshare Owner's Guide to Winning the Timeshare Game

Published in the United States by TimeshareGame.com

Portions of this book may also be incorporated in website and training
materials made available through TimeshareGame.com.

First Edition

Designed by Deanna Keahey

Library of Congress Cataloguing in Publication Data has been applied
for.

ISBN - 978-0-9888392-3-6

"You have to learn the rules of the game, and then you need to play better than anyone else."

~ Albert Einstein

Table of Contents

8. Option B2 - Exchanging with Interval   133

9. Option C - Multiplying Your Vacations   168

Introduction

Who is this book for?

Does your timeshare fail to live up to your hopes and expectations? Do you wish your timeshare gave you more bang for your buck? This book was written to help you, the timeshare owner, get the most possible value from your timeshare.

It's unfortunate, but many owners spent a lot of money on a timeshare, and aren't getting nearly as much value as they expected. They find it frustrating and difficult to get the vacations they want, and they aren't sure what to do about it. Some people end up just taking whatever they can get, settling for a vacation that wasn't what they hoped for. In other cases, disillusioned owners have given up on their timeshare, yet they're stuck paying the bills and they still owe a bundle on it. What a shame!

This book is dedicated to the proposition that timeshares can be a lot of fun, and that people who own them deserve to get the maximum vacation value for the money they pay.

This book is for you if...

* If you're a new timeshare owner, who's just learning the ropes. You envision many fun vacations, and you're wondering about the optimal way to arrange things. I'll explain all the different ways you can use your timeshare, and go into detail about how to get the best reservations and exchanges. You'll soon have a clear picture of your possibilities, and know the next steps to take.

* If you've gotten enjoyment from using your timeshare, but wonder if there are other benefits you might be missing out on, I'm going to show you all the different options you have for getting value from your ownership. This can open your eyes to opportunities you didn't even know about.

Jerry owned his timeshare in Hilton Head for years, and he was pretty happy with it. He used it a few years, and other years exchanged it to vacation in other places. One day a friend was talking about timeshares, and tipped him off to a couple of techniques. When Jerry got home, he did some checking, and discovered that he could get almost twice the trading power he'd been getting before. After making a few changes, Jerry now gets double the vacations for the same price. Sweet!

Are you getting the most out of your timeshare, or is there more you could do?

❋ If you've heard other people talk about exchanging their timeshares but you aren't really sure how this works or what to do, I'll walk you through the different avenues for exchanging your timeshare, showing you how to maximize your value and get the best possible exchanges.

❋ If you bought a timeshare and feel like you were sold a bill of goods because you haven't been able to use it like you thought you could, I'll explain what your options for it are now. A lot of the value comes down to knowing what you can do, and how to do it. This book can provide the information you need, without any hype, spin or pressure.

Sandra has a timeshare in Cancun that she bought 8 years ago. The past few years she hasn't been able to make the trip due to work and health issues, and it's been sitting there unused. It's a waste to keep paying the fees every year, and she wishes she never got into this mess. She doesn't know what else to do. She's just hoping that next year will be different.

If you're frustrated with your timeshare, this book can help!

❋ If you are considering buying a timeshare and want to know more before you make the commitment, this book will give you a wealth of insights into what timeshare ownership entails and what you can expect, so that you can make an informed, intelligent decision about whether to buy.

* If you would like to learn how to multiply your vacations, so that owning just one timeshare can get you many vacations, I'm going to explain how timeshare owners can vacation for multiple weeks (or even months) each year, without investing in any additional timeshares. There are even people who do timesharing full-time using these techniques.

* If you like saving money and getting great bargains on vacations, but consider your existing timeshare trips fairly pricey, I'll show you some ways that you can get vacations for prices that are so low it's almost unbelievable.

* If family, work, or other commitments mean that you cannot use your timeshare right now, I will lay out different ways that you can still get value from your timeshare. Just because you can't use it doesn't mean it needs to go to waste.

* If you are concerned about some of the pitfalls that can be a problem for timeshare owners, I discuss ownership issues that can arise, how they could affect you, and what you can do about them.

* If you enjoy the timeshare you own, and are thinking of expanding your timeshare portfolio, I walk you through the pros and cons of different approaches, and considerations to keep in mind when designing your portfolio.

Where should you start?

Most people won't want or need to read this book from beginning to end.

Some sections apply only to certain timeshares. For example, if you own a timeshare week, you don't need the chapters on points. Other sections apply only in particular situations, like the chapter on multiplying your vacations, if you have the free time to enjoy that.

Here's what you will find in this book, so that you can choose the parts most applicable for your needs.

☑ *Chapter 1 - You've Got Options* presents an overview of the different things you can do with your timeshare, such as using it yourself, exchanging it, renting it out, or turning it into multiple weeks. This is an overview, with details following in later chapters.

☑ *Chapter 2 - Understanding What You Own* is about gaining a full understanding of the different elements of your timeshare. As timeshare systems have gotten more complex over the years, this is no longer as straightforward as it sounds, and I walk you through different parameters and situations. Understanding what you own is the foundation for everything else that follows.

☑ *Chapter 3 - Option A: Using Your Timeshare*. Chapters 3-5 are all about using your own timeshare. This chapter in particular talks about general considerations for using your own timeshare, no matter what you own. Whether you have weeks or points, the tips and techniques in this section will be useful for you.

☑ *Chapter 4 - Option A1: Using Your Week*. If you own a timeshare week, rather than points, then this section will give you the strategies and tactics you need in order to get the best vacations when you use it yourself.

☑ *Chapter 5 - Option A2 - Using Your Points*. If you own points rather than a straight timeshare week, then making the best use of your ownership requires some different techniques. This chapter explains what you need to know to get the best vacations with your points.

☑ *Chapter 6 - Option B: Exchanging Your Timeshare*. Chapters 6-8 are all about exchanging or trading your timeshare to stay somewhere else. This chapter goes through your different options for exchanging. Many people are not even aware of all the opportunities they have. Just because RCI and Interval International are the largest exchange companies, does not mean they are your only choices.

☑ *Chapter 7 - Option B1, Exchanging with RCI*, is for you if your timeshare is associated with RCI, the largest timeshare exchange company in the world. This is where you'll find details on how to maximize your trading power and get the best exchanges for your timeshare using this popular system.

☑ *Chapter 8 - Option B2, Exchanging with Interval*, is for you if your timeshare is associated with Interval International (II), the other major exchange company. This chapter will show you the techniques you need to maximize your exchange success with II. You'll also discover Interval's secret program that gives you an extra vacation week for every exchange you make. Sound interesting?

☑ *Chapter 9 - Option C, Multiplying Your Vacations* delves into all the ways you can turn one week of timeshare ownership or a fixed number of points, into many more weeks of vacation. If you have the time to travel, this chapter will open your eyes to new ways you can get more vacations for less money.

☑ *Chapter 10 - Option D, Taking Fewer Vacations* is intended to help you out in those situations where you can't use your timeshare yourself. Whether it's a health issue or work commitments getting in the way, sometimes this happens. This chapter provides a wealth of details about how to save it, rent it, or use it in different ways, so that you still get the maximum value from your timeshare even when you can't take that vacation.

☑ *Chapter 11 - Advanced Tactics & Evaluating Options* discusses more complex timeshare strategies and techniques. Find out how to weigh different options to see which gives you the most value. For instance, is it better to use your own timeshare, or to deposit it with an exchange company, and then trade back into your own resort? You may be surprised by what's possible.

☑ *Chapter 12 - How the Finances Work* discusses the monetary aspects of owning a timeshare, and using it in different ways. You'll find out how to calculate the true cost of your ownership and the timeshare vacations you take. When you are evaluating options, it is important to have a reliable way to calculate and compare the costs, and this chapter shows you how to do that.

☑ *Chapter 13 - Creating Your Timeshare Calendar* walks you through building a plan to optimize the timing of your timeshare activities. Doing things at the right time is a major factor in being able to get the most value and enjoyment from your timeshare. This chapter goes into detail about setting up your personal timeshare calendar, and creating a working system for your ongoing activities.

☑ *Chapter 14 - Potential Ownership Issues* covers some of the complications that may arise when you own a timeshare. Some are almost ubiquitous (such as rising fees), while others (like company mergers) are less frequent. If you own a timeshare, it is wise to be aware of what can happen, and what you can do about it.

☑ *Chapter 15 - Your Timeshare Portfolio* discusses points to consider and evaluate when you are making the decision to purchase another timeshare. This chapter is for timeshare aficionados who want to be smart about planning their vacation ownership, rather than just buying what a salesperson wants to sell them.

☑ *Chapter 16 - Additional Resources*. This is where you will find a useful *Timeshare glossary* in case you run into any unfamiliar jargon. You will also find lists of helpful timeshare organizations and resources, with links for their websites.

No matter what sort of timeshare you own, or how many weeks or points you have, wouldn't it be nice to know that you are always getting the most benefit from it? Wouldn't it be nice to know exactly what you can do, and feel like you have mastered the system?

After reading this book, you will understand all the different ways that you can use your timeshare, and have the necessary knowledge of what to do, how to do it, and when to do it.

Your attitude towards your timeshare could change dramatically, once you can make better use of it. The quality of your vacations can go up, while the cost goes down. Soon, you'll be telling friends about the great timeshare vacation deal you just got, and they'll all want to know how you did it.

You'll be able to relax, knowing that you are ahead of the game, rather than feeling like somebody has put one over on you. That's when you know you're Winning the Timeshare Game.

Using the worksheets

For your convenience, and to help you plan and manage your timeshare activities as effectively as possible, this book comes with a number of complimentary timeshare worksheets. These are all downloadable worksheets provided in Excel format.

Make the most of your timeshare. Staying organized and on top of all your timeshare activities can really help you make the most of it, ensuring that you always have the information you need, take action at the optimal times, and never miss a deadline. These worksheets are designed to help you do just that.

Save time, track efficiently. These expertly designed worksheets can save you many hours that you could otherwise spend putting together your own system. It is much easier to use this proven system than to try to figure it out on your own, going through revision after revision as you discover something else to include. These worksheets give you a jump start, with a proven system that's ready to go.

Optional, but useful. If you want to keep track of your timeshare activities, then these worksheets will certainly be useful. However, not everyone wants or needs to use tracking spreadsheets. If your situation is very straightforward, you may only need a couple of these, or perhaps you're just not a spreadsheet person. No problem. Just pick and choose what seems useful for you.

Here's a quick overview of the spreadsheets provided with this book.

☑   _Worksheet A - Timeshare Info Sheet_. This worksheet gives you a handy place to note the key details about your timeshare. This documents exactly what you own, with account numbers, deed information, purchase details, and more. Whether you own one timeshare or several, this worksheet will handle it.

☑   _Worksheet B - Using Your Timeshare_. This worksheet holds everything you need to know about using your own timeshare. When and how can you book your reservation? Are there deadlines or target dates for taking action? Do you have favorite units, and who do you contact to request those? When you want to make a reservation, this sheet has everything you need, and it can cover multiple timeshares.

☑ *Worksheet C - Tracking Points*. If you have timeshare points, this worksheet helps you plan and track all of your points activities. You can see what points you have available, use years and expiration dates, vacations booked, and activities such as borrowing, saving, and extending points. It can cover multiple timeshares and different points systems.

☑ *Worksheet D - Tracking RCI Exchanges*.

☑ *Worksheet E - Tracking II Exchanges*.

These last two worksheets help you plan, manage and track your exchange activities. You can see what you have deposited, what searches are in progress, what vacations you have booked, critical expiration dates, and fees paid. Because the RCI and II systems operate quite differently, the tracking spreadsheets are different for the two systems. The II worksheet can also be used to track your activities if you use any of the smaller exchange companies.

Important notes

Notations used

Throughout the book, you will see these notations that mark important pieces of information:

Expert tips: These are expert tips from timeshare owners with years of experience. Taking advantage of these tips can save you money, time, and headaches.

Learn more: These are additional web resources that offer in-depth information on a topic. You can dig deeper and learn more about this topic by following the link.

Watch out: These are problems, pitfalls or scams that you may run into which can cost you money or impact your ability to use your timeshare. Watch out for these situations.

Additional notes

Many different rules. There are many different timeshares out there, all of which have their own different rules. This book discusses numerous variations, with examples of how certain things are handled with different companies. However, each company, or even each resort, can have its own rules. It is important that you verify the rules for your own timeshare. The worksheets give you a handy place to note those details for easy reference later.

Changing rules. The timeshare industry is known for changing the rules and introducing new twists. Everything in this book was researched as of the publication date, but be aware that every company has its own rules, and many rules may change over time.

Prices. All prices in the book are quoted in US dollars, and are subject to change. Fees will vary in different countries (it's not necessarily a straight currency conversion), and prices can change at any time.

This is not legal or financial advice. The author of this book is not a lawyer or an accountant, and this book does not offer any legal or financial advice. If you have questions about the law or require legal counsel, consult an attorney familiar with timeshare law. If you have questions that pertain to your finances, consult an accountant or financial planner.

Can you help? If you see anything that's outdated, missing, or just plain wrong in this book, can you please help? I've tried to make it as complete and accurate as possible, but things change continually, and there's always a possibility that I missed something. If you have any additions, corrections, comments, or questions, please leave them at *TimeshareGame.com/contact-us/*

Thanks!

1. You've Got Options

Once you are a timeshare owner, you have vacation opportunities you didn't have before, but many owners don't know about all of their options, or how to use them. Some timeshare owners are frustrated and unhappy because they can't make good use of their timeshare. Others manage to get many wonderful vacations from their ownership. It all comes down to knowing what you can do, and how to do it.

Here's a sampling of what you can do with a timeshare.

* **Take economical family vacations**. Stay in a fully furnished condo that's large enough for your entire family, and enjoy a comfortable, economical, and fun vacation.

* **Guarantee your favorite resort every summer**. Stay at your favorite place every summer, even though it could be totally unavailable to the general public. You've got your vacation locked in, where you want and when you want.

* **Visit a different destination every year**. If you want more variety, you can exchange your timeshare for resort vacations around the world. Want to try Hawaii this year? The Caribbean? Italy? It's all possible.

* **Get incredible deals on discount vacations**. There are unbelievable prices available on resort vacations, if you watch for them and are able to move fast. How about a ski resort for less than $30/night? Yes, it's possible.

* **Rent it or give it**. If you don't want to use your timeshare one year, you can rent it out for some extra cash. Or, if it's your parents' 50th anniversary, you could give them a vacation as an extra special gift.

* **Multiply your vacations**. You can leverage your timeshare to provide multiple weeks of vacation per year, when you know the ins and outs of how to make the most of it. Soon, your friends may get jealous, asking "Where are you going now?"

Read on to find out more about your options, and how to make the most of your timeshare.

Overview of your timeshare options

Option A - Using your own timeshare

When you bought your timeshare, chances are you did it because you loved the resort where you bought. You could visualize yourself and your family enjoying happy vacations there, and found the other properties in the system appealing. Your first option is to use your own timeshare (either weeks or points), staying at the resort you bought, or using the same company's points system.

There are some definite advantages to using your own timeshare. For more on this, and a detailed guide to using your own timeshare most effectively, look at chapters

▸ *Option A - Using Your Timeshare* (general tips for both weeks and points)

▸ *Option A1 - Using Your Week*

▸ *Option A2 - Using Your Points*

Expert tip: Using hybrid timeshares. If you own a hybrid week/points timeshare, sometimes your timeshare will act like a week and other times it will act like points. See *Weeks, points and hybrid systems*. If you own a timeshare like this, then read all of the above sections to learn how to work your timeshare both ways.

Option B - Exchanging your timeshare

No matter how much you love your own timeshare, there will be times when you'd like to get away to somewhere else. Perhaps you've always wanted to visit New York City, the Cayman Islands, or the coast of Spain, and your timeshare system doesn't have any properties there. Or perhaps you just enjoy exploring some place new for a change. Exchanging your timeshare is a way to do this.

You're not tied to vacationing at your own resort or one of the resorts affiliated with your timeshare system. Exchange companies give you access to thousands of other properties around the world. There are various timeshare exchange companies out there, and they each function a bit differently. Knowing how to use them most effectively will maximize your chances of getting the vacation you want.

To learn how to work the system for your maximum benefit when exchanging your timeshare, see the chapters

‣ _Option B - Exchanging Your Timeshare_ (general tips for all exchanges)

‣ _Option B1 - Exchanging with RCI_

‣ _Option B2 - Exchanging with Interval_

Option C - Multiplying your vacations

Do you know how many ways there are to expand your timeshare vacations at excellent prices? Even if you own just a single week, that doesn't mean you're limited to just one week of timeshare vacation. You could spend weeks or months traveling the world and staying at different timeshares, without buying any additional timeshare yourself.

If you've got the time and want more vacations, find out all about different ways to leverage your timeshare and travel more, in chapter

‣ _Option C - Multiplying Your Vacations_

Option D - Taking fewer vacations

As much as we all enjoy holidays, things don't always work out. Sometimes business demands, family issues or health complications pose obstacles. Even if you can't get away to travel, you still have options so your timeshare doesn't go to waste.

When you can't use your timeshare to take a vacation, find out about all the other ways you can still extract value from it, in chapter

‣ *Option D - Taking Fewer Vacations*

2. Understanding What You Own

Timeshare fundamentals

Timeshares used to be pretty simple. The basic concept was that you could split the ownership of a vacation property with a number of other like-minded people.

The simplest version of timesharing is buying a fixed unit (e.g. unit #423, a 2-bedroom ocean view condo), for a fixed period of time (e.g. week #26 each year). As an owner, this would entitle you to use your specific unit on your specific week each year. This type of timeshare system is less common than it used to be, though you can still find some out there.

The timeshare industry has evolved since then and created a number of different systems. The general trend has been toward greater flexibility, but at the cost of increased complexity. As new innovations continue to be introduced, they combine to make the seemingly simple question of "what exactly do you own?" more complicated than you'd expect.

Here are some of the key elements to understand about the timeshare you own. Knowing how these fundamentals apply to your specific timeshare is critical for you to make the most effective use of it.

Weeks, Points, and Hybrid systems

Weeks. In a system based on weeks, you buy the right to use a timeshare unit at a specific resort for a week each year. Buying a week gets you a 7-night vacation at this resort.

A week is the most common time interval, but it can vary in some ownership systems. You might have a timeshare that gives you 2 weeks a year, a month a year, or a week every other year. The principle is the same - you're buying a vacation interval that corresponds to a little slice of that resort.

If you love vacationing at this resort every year, this is an ideal arrangement. But what if you like to switch things around sometimes? You're covered on this, too.

When you're tired of staying at your own resort and ready for a change, you can exchange your week to stay at a different resort. Exchange companies give you access to other resorts around the world. (This is a big topic, covered starting in *Option B - Exchanging Your Timeshare*.)

Points. Most of the major timeshare systems have now switched to a points system instead of selling weeks. Rather than buying *"1 week,"* you might by *"50,000 points."* The actual number of points that corresponds to one week varies widely, depending on what system you're in, and how desirable the resort, unit and week are.

Points are like timeshare money. You use your points to book vacation time at one of the resorts that is part of your system. For instance, if you own points in the Worldmark system, there is a list of resorts where you can use your Worldmark points.

Unlike owning a week, points systems let you stay for shorter amounts of time. If a 7-night vacation stay doesn't fit your schedule, you could spend 3 nights one place, and take a 4-night vacation somewhere else later. You would just pay for each of those stays with an appropriate number of points.

You can also vacation farther afield, visiting resorts that are outside your system. Just like you can exchange a timeshare week to stay at other resorts, there are ways to exchange your points-based timeshare, too.

Hybrid Systems. Not everything is as simple as Weeks or Points, since there are hybrid timeshare systems that combine elements of both.

For instance, if you own an RCI Points timeshare, you actually own a timeshare week at a particular resort. Someone (either you or a previous owner) paid to "convert" this to RCI Points, so that you can use RCI's points-based system.

In this example, you own a hybrid timeshare - you have both a week and points. You have options on how to use your timeshare - either as a week or as points, depending on what actions you take at specific times. You'll find more on all of this later! For now, just make sure you know whether you own a week, points, or a hybrid of both.

Chart - Popular timeshare systems

The chart below includes some of the most popular timeshare systems in the US, showing how they normally work as far as weeks vs. points. There are a couple of reasons that this isn't always clear cut.

* **Changes over time**. Some timeshare systems have changed how they work over the years. For instance, the Marriott Vacation Club is a points-based system, but Marriott used to sell weeks, so some Marriott owners have points while others have weeks.

* **Ownership changes.** Some resorts have been owned by different companies over time. For example, Diamond Resorts is a points system, but they took over a number of resorts that used to be Sunterra properties. Some owners at these properties joined the Diamond points system, while others still own the timeshare weeks they purchased when it was Sunterra.

As you can see, this gets complicated!

The chart below covers the normal situations, but due to the reasons above, you may find specific cases that differ from the norm. Also, there are timeshares that are not part of the systems on this list.

Company	How it works
Bluegreen Vacation Club (BVC)	You have a points package, which is backed by a deeded specific unit and week.
Diamond Resorts International (DRI)	Points are usually attached to a specific "Collection" of resorts. Some Diamond owners have a deeded week, which may or may not have associated points.
Disney Vacation Club (DVC)	You own points, with a right to use interest in a specific resort. There is an expiration date.
Hilton Grand Vacation Club (HGVC)	You own a week in a particular property and season, which gives you a certain number of points.
Marriott Vacation Club (MVC)	The Destination Club is a points-based system. Some people own Marriott weeks, as mentioned earlier.
RCI Points	You own a week at a particular resort and season, which has been converted to RCI Points.
Starwood Vacation Ownership (SVO)	You own a deeded week, which may or may not also give you a certain number of Staroption points.
Vacation Resorts International (VRI)	You own a week at a particular resort. Some VRI weeks have also been converted to RCI Points.
Westgate Resorts	You own a fixed or floating deeded week in a particular resort and season.

Company	How it works
Worldmark, The Club	You own points in the club. The deeded real estate is owned by the club.
Wyndham (Club Wyndham)	You may own points backed by a deeded week, or non-deeded points (Club Wyndham Access).

We'll delve into all the details of how to use your weeks and/or points in upcoming sections of the book. For now, just make sure you understand what type of ownership you have.

Annual, Biennial, Triennial

This means how often you get to use your timeshare. Annual usage is the most common, but there are other variations.

Annual. This is straightforward, and it's the most common type of plan. You get to use your timeshare (whether it's a week or points) every year. You also pay the maintenance fee every year, though it may be split into monthly payments.

Biennial. With a biennial timeshare, you get the usage of your timeshare (either a week or points) every other year, instead of every single year. It's a fairly common way to allow people to get into timesharing for a lower cost of ownership than buying an Annual timeshare.

Biennial is often referred to as **EOY** (for Every Other Year). You'll also see it listed as Odd Years or Even Years, to indicate which years you can use it.

This seemingly simple concept can get a bit complicated in some systems. Let's say you own an Odd Years timeshare. Here are some ways it could work, depending on the system you're in.

- Use your timeshare (either a week or points) only in Odd years, and pay all your fees only in those same years.

- Use your timeshare only in Odd years, but pay half your fees every year.

- Receive half your points every year, and pay half your fees every year.

- Receive all your points in the Odd years, but half expire after one year, and the other half expire after two years.

If you own a Biennial or EOY timeshare, you need to know how the system works at your timeshare, in order to plan effectively and make the most of your ownership.

Triennial. This is similar to Biennial, but instead of getting usage of your timeshare every other year, you get usage of it every third year. This is less common than Annual or Biennial.

Unit types

If you own a timeshare week, or own in a hybrid system, then you also own a certain type of unit. This is most commonly specified by size, but can be broken out further as well.

If you own in a pure points system, then you don't own a specific type of unit, but you'll be using your points to purchase stays in units of these types.

Unit size. From smallest to largest, here are the normal unit sizes you'll encounter.

* **Hotel**. Some timeshares are basically hotels that have been converted to a different type of ownership. Just like in a hotel room, you'll have one or two beds in a single room, plus a bathroom. There's no kitchen, but there may be a small refrigerator or microwave.

* **Studio**. Similar to a studio apartment, this type of unit will give you a combined bedroom / living room / dining area. You'll generally have kitchen facilities, though it may be a limited kitchen.

Learn more: Unit type variations. This seems simple, but unit sizes aren't always what you would expect. Find out more in _When is a studio not a studio?_ at _TimeshareGame.com/owners-guide-links/_

* **1-Bedroom**. In this type of unit, you have one private bedroom which is separate from the living / dining area. The living room may have a pull-out sofa bed to accommodate more people. There is usually a full kitchen, or at least a partial kitchen.

* **2-Bedroom**. You guessed it... Two bedrooms, plus a living / dining area, with a full kitchen. This is the most common size for US timeshares. Usually, the living room also has a pull-out sofa bed. Sometimes there are two living room areas, each with a pull-out bed.

* **3+ Bedroom**. Some resorts offer larger units with 3 or 4 bedrooms. These larger units are relatively uncommon, so if you have a sizable group of people, you may need to book two smaller units.

Sleeping capacity / Private capacity. Each unit has a fixed number of people it can accommodate. The sleeping capacity is the maximum number of people who can stay there. The private capacity is often a smaller number, meaning the number who can sleep there with privacy. For instance, a 2-bedroom unit with a fold-out couch in the living room could have sleeping capacity 6 and private capacity 4, since the living room is not private.

Lock-off Units. A Lock-off unit (sometimes referred to as a Lock-out) is a large unit that can be split into two smaller units with a locking door in between. Each of the smaller units has its own keyed entry and its own facilities. This means that each can be used independently of the other, or you can use the full combined unit all together.

For instance, you might own a 2-bedroom unit which can be split into a 1-bedroom + a studio. You can find more about using Lock-offs in the sections on _Splitting your unit for double the fun_, and _Maximizing your RCI trading power_.

Unit subtype. At some resorts, all units of a certain size are categorized the same, but other places have them broken out further based on desirability. Here are a few examples.

* **Type of view**. The view often makes some units more desirable than others, for instance Ocean View vs. Garden View.

* **Location**. Some locations may be worth more than others, such as Ocean Front vs. non, or upper floors vs. lower.

* **Deluxe, Chalet, etc.** There may be different unit configurations in the same size range, so that you might have a 1-Bedroom Deluxe, 1-Bedroom Chalet, 1-Bedroom Standard, etc.

Fixed vs. Floating weeks

When you own a timeshare week, both the unit and the time period can be fixed or floating.

Fixed Units. Fixed means you own the right to stay in the same unit from year to year. For instance, you might own unit #234, and you'll always be in the same place, every year.

Floating Units. With this type of ownership, you have the right to use a particular type of unit each time you visit, rather than the same exact unit. For instance, you might own a 2-bedroom unit. When you visit, you get assigned to any available unit of this type at the resort.

Fixed Week. A fixed week gives you the right to use your unit for a specific time period each year. For instance, you might own week 31 each year (where week 1 is the first week in the year). This would put your week in early August, ideal for a family vacation each summer when the kids are out of school. You would be locked into the same week each year.

Floating Week. Instead of owning a fixed week, owning a floating week means you can select from weeks during a given season. For instance, you might own a Summer week, usable any time from June through August. You could use it in July one year, and August the next.

If you own a floating week, there are different ways that time slots may be allocated to owners, but the most common is first-come, first-served. If you own a Summer week and want to be there over the 4th of July, then you need to move quickly to get what you want. Seasons and weeks are commonly color coded to indicate demand.

Timeshare seasons

Most resorts have the year broken into different seasons, based on patterns of demand. High season is when the most people want to stay there, and it costs more this time of year. Low or Off season has the lowest demand, and is the cheapest. Mid or Shoulder season is in between.

Definitions vary by location. The calendar for each resort determines which weeks fall into which seasons. February could be High season at a ski resort, and Low season at a beach resort. It all depends on the demand - when do the most people want to visit?

Color coding. Timeshare seasons are often color coded to indicate demand. Different companies use different color codes, which can be confusing. A common designation is that Red = High season. Thus, you'll frequently see "Red week" to indicate a floating week in the prime season. Other companies use Platinum to designate their highest season.

Seasons with weeks. When you buy a floating week, you buy into one of these seasons. People pay less up-front to purchase a week in Low season than in High season. When you exchange, rent, or sell your timeshare week, High season will always be worth more than Low season.

Learn more: Seasonal ownership issues. If you are an owner at a seasonal resort, find out more about how the season you own affects you in _Timeshare Issues - The Blue Week Blues_. The more seasonal your resort, the more important this is. See _TimeshareGame.com/owners-guide-links/_

Expert tip: Year round red. Some resorts consider every week of the year to be a red week. This is the case with many resorts in Hawaii, Las Vegas, and some other places. While it's true that people do like to visit Hawaii year round, it's not really true that demand is the same every week of the year. For instance, families with kids in school can only vacation during school holidays, which creates a significant shift in demand. Though all the weeks are labeled "Red," some weeks are "Redder" than others, and will be more difficult to book.

There may be exclusions. Sometimes specific weeks (especially holiday weeks) are excluded from the normal season calendar. Due to the very high demand for those specific weeks, they may be handled as fixed weeks, even in a floating calendar. For example, high season might not include Christmas week. If you own high season, you could go the week before or after Christmas, but not that specific week.

Seasons with points. If you own points rather than weeks, then the seasons still apply, but operate differently. You own a fixed number of points, and can spend them when you want. It will cost you more points to stay during high season than it will during low season. You might be able to get a large unit for a full week in low season, but only a smaller unit or shorter stay in high season.

Expert tip: Escalating seasons. Low season seems to be shrinking, as companies escalate the seasons. You'll find that some timeshare companies list 4 seasons such as Low / Mid / High / Peak, with no dates falling into Low. In effect, you end up with the same three seasons, but now they're called Mid / High / Peak. It doesn't make much sense to have "Mid" at the bottom of the list, taking the dates that obviously are really low season. Perhaps it's their way to make those low season dates sound more appealing, or perhaps they can charge more if they don't call them "Low."

Deeded ownership vs. Right to Use

Deeded Unit. When you own a deeded timeshare, you actually own a portion of a timeshare property and have a legal deed for it. You own this forever, just like you would own other real estate, though the contract may just give you ownership of part of the resort, not any of the land on which the timeshare is built. You pay real estate taxes on this property (often bundled into the annual maintenance fee), and you can pass it on to your heirs. Deeded ownership is sometimes called "fee simple."

There are different ways that a deeded timeshare can work:

Deeded and fixed. Your deed may say that you own a specific unit and specific interval. For instance, you own might own unit #216 for week 42 each year. In a fixed unit / fixed week system, this means you get to use exactly what your deed says you own.

Deeded and floating. Your deed might say that you have a type of unit, rather than a specific unit. For instance, you might own a 2-bedroom ocean view unit for week 17 each year. It's not a specific unit number, just a certain type of unit.

Expert tip: Deed may not match what you get to use. There may be a difference between what your deed says and what you actually get to use. It's not uncommon for a deed to show a specific week, while your timeshare contract gives you a floating week. For example, you might have a deed that lists a "*1-Bedroom Unit, week 11,*" but it also mentions "*Annual usage Platinum ski season.*" In this case, what really matters for using your timeshare is the "*Annual usage Platinum ski season.*" The "*week 11*" on your deed is more for record keeping, and will be useful when you decide to sell your timeshare, or if you own more than one timeshare at the same resort.

Undivided Interest. In this case, you own a tiny fraction of the resort, but it's a non-specific interest. Rather than owning unit #309 for week 37, you might own 0.0302% of the undivided total resort. This may be combined with a right to use contract. For instance, you might own 0.0302% undivided interest, along with the right to use a 2-Bedroom Ocean View unit for one week per year during Prime Season, or points that give you an equivalent benefit.

Right to Use. With a pure Right to Use contract, you do not actually own any real estate, and there is no deed. Instead, you'll have a "Certifi*cate of Ownership*" or similar document, that says you own certain rights to use the property (or properties). With right to use timeshares, you may still have to pay an allocated share of property taxes, which will normally be included in your maintenance fee.

A Right to Use contract may have an expiration date. For example, you could have the right to use a 2-bedroom unit for one week each year, for the next 25 years. At the end of that 25 year period, all rights would revert to the property owner.

Expert tip: Expiration date pros and cons. Having an expiration date isn't always a bad thing. Of course, it does mean that you don't actually own your timeshare forever, and your ability to sell it, or will it to kids or grandkids, will disappear in time. On the other hand, the obligation to make maintenance payments will also disappear in time, which may be a good thing!

Vacation Club. A vacation club is normally a right to use arrangement, where you don't own a resort property, but rather buy a club membership that gives you the right to use several different resorts. The club is run by trustees who control the resort properties.

Expert tip: Combinations. Either Weeks or Points can be Deeded or Right to Use. For example, you can buy into a vacation club that gives you a deed to a share in the undivided real property at a resort, together with a set of points that you use to book your holiday stays.

Home week, Home resort, Home group

Depending on the timeshare you own, these terms may or may not be applicable to you. Here's a rundown on what they mean and how they normally work.

Home week. If you own a specific week at a specific resort, then this is your "*Home week.*" In a fixed timeshare system, this is the week that you can use for your vacation. If you decide to exchange your week to vacation somewhere else, this same week is the week you would use for exchanging.

If you own in a hybrid weeks / points system, then you may also have a home week. In this case, you'll have an option of using your home week yourself, or taking the associated points and spending them to book your vacation.

Home resort. If you own any fixed or floating week at a specific resort, then this is your "*Home resort.*" If you have a resort name listed on your deed, that is your home resort. You have certain usage rights at this resort, based on what you own. Your maintenance fees will be based on the budget for this resort.

You usually get preferential booking privileges at your home resort. For instance, the Hilton Grand Vacation Club is a hybrid weeks / points system. You own a week at your home resort, and that week is assigned a certain number of points. If you want to stay at your home resort, you can book that vacation (for the season and unit type you own) up to 12 months in advance. People who are part of the Hilton club but own at a different resort must wait until 9 months before the check-in date to book a stay at your home resort. Your home resort ownership means you get first shot at the dates you want.

Home group. Depending on what system you're in, you may also be part of a "*Home group.*" This is a group of resorts that are all affiliated with your home resort, and it may also be called a "Collection." This can be useful for getting bookings at resorts that are part of your home group. For instance, with RCI Points, you can book at any resort in your home group up to 11 months before the check-in date. People who are not part of your home group must wait until 10 months prior to check-in, to book the same thing with their RCI points.

Worksheet A - Timeshare Info Sheet

Summary

This worksheet gathers fundamental information about your timeshare, including all of the items discussed in this section.

Having your timeshare details documented like this provides great clarity, and means you don't have to dig through your files when you have a question about it.

How to use this worksheet

- **Timeshare at a glance** - Summary section with the most commonly used timeshare information.

- **Resort / Company info** - Key details such as address, website, and phone number. If you own at a specific resort, this will be resort information. If you own pure points, this would be company information.

- **Ownership details - Weeks** - Information on weeks ownership, such as unit type, season owned, weeks you can use it, and check-in days.

- **Ownership details - Points** - Information on points ownership, such as number of points owned and use year start date. This is also where you can note the rules for your system on saving, borrowing, renting and transferring points. (See more about those in *Working with points*.)

- **Ownership details - Deeded** - If you own a deeded timeshare, this has details such as the deed number, and where and when it was recorded.

- **Purchase details** - Information about the purchase such as the date, price, closing and other costs, where and from whom it was purchased, and how long the process took.

- **Initial usage details** - When the timeshare is first available for your use, when the first maintenance fees are due, and how much that will be.

Usage tips

- **Keep a hard copy with paperwork** - Since the data on this worksheet is static, I like to print this out and keep it in a binder or file together with the original timeshare documents, as well as any important correspondence, notices from the resort, etc.

- **Use selected sections** - Depending on what you own (e.g. weeks or points, deeded or not), just use whichever sections of this worksheet are applicable.

- **Multiple timeshares** - If you own more than one timeshare, you can add another tab to the Excel workbook so that you have a separate worksheet for each timeshare you own.

Links to worksheets

- SAMPLE worksheet - This copy is filled out with sample data for different types of timeshares. The data is not real - it's purely for illustration purposes, so you can see how the spreadsheet works.

- BLANK worksheet - For your own use.

- Worksheets are at
  TimeshareGame.com/owners-guide-links/

3. Option A - Using Your Timeshare

Advantages of staying at your own timeshare

Booking your vacation at your home resort, or in your own timeshare system, offers some distinct advantages.

Priority reservations. In most timeshare systems, you get a head start on bookings for your home resort. Owners usually get a month or more lead time before bookings are available for non-owners. If you own at a highly desirable resort or want to vacation there during a peak week, this priority reservation can make all the difference between getting what you want or not.

No exchange fee required. When you stay at your own timeshare, you don't have to pay an exchange fee. For instance, if you're dealing with RCI (the largest exchange company), you could save $219* compared to the cost of exchanging your timeshare to stay elsewhere. *(*All fees subject to change.)*

No additional membership fee. If you only want to stay at your own timeshare, and are not interested in exchanges or extra vacations (more on those later), then you don't need to pay the annual membership fee for an exchange company. This could save you $89-124 a year.
Note: Some timeshare systems give you an automatic membership that's rolled into your maintenance fees, in which case there is no way to avoid it.

Fewer extra resort fees. In an effort to increase their revenues, a lot of resorts are charging add-on fees such as registration fees, housekeeping fees, and daily resort fees. In many cases, these extra fees only apply to outsiders staying at the property, while the timeshare owners don't have to pay them.

Simpler process. If you want to use your own week, or book a vacation with your own points, it is a relatively simple process. If you want to stay elsewhere, you can do that via an exchange company, but it's a more complicated process that can take months.

Standardized level of accommodation. For example, if you're an owner with the Marriott Vacation Club, you probably bought there because you enjoy staying in resorts with a certain quality level. As long as you stay within the Marriott system, you can be confident the places you stay will meet your quality criteria. If you exchange to one of the thousands of other timeshares out there, you'll need to do more research to get a resort that meets your expectations.

You know the place. If you stay at the same resort over multiple years, you get to know the place. You know the resort layout and what to expect from the facilities and amenities. You know the front desk staff, your favorite restaurants in the area, and where the closest grocery store is. It feels familiar, almost like a second home, rather than just another place to go.

Building friendships. If you visit your home resort at the same time each year, you're apt to meet other people who do, too. You may end up making friends with other families who visit at the same time, and meet them year after year.

Specifics on fees and booking priority vary in different timeshares. In general, though, there are significant advantages to staying at your own timeshare.

Make plans early

Many owners new to timesharing don't realize how important it is to act early in making your vacation plans. Planning one or more years ahead is a different mindset for a lot of people, and it does take some getting used to.

Unless you own a fixed week, then even at your home resort, your chances of getting the vacation dates you want depend on when you book your reservation. Here are some pointers you need to know.

Book as early as possible. The best way to get what you want is to book your reservations as soon as you can. Most floating week and points timeshare systems are booked on a first come, first served basis (within certain parameters). Whoever books soonest gets first dibs on the choice weeks, so the sooner you can make your plans, the better off you will be.

Know your earliest booking date. Different companies and resorts have different rules about how far in advance you can make a reservation, so make sure you know the rules for your timeshare.

For example, some resorts open up reservations 2 years in advance for owners at that resort. People who book 2 years in advance will get first pick of the dates they want. If you are slower to act and don't make a reservation until 6 months beforehand, your selections will be limited.

Expert tip - Paying fees early can pay off. Many timeshares (but not all) won't let you make a reservation for a year before you've paid your maintenance fees for that same year. If you want to book 2 years in advance, you need to pay your fees 2 years in advance. The downside is obvious, but the pay-off is that you get the best reservation opportunities. Paying ahead the first time you do it is a financial burden, but once you're on a "pay 2 years in advance" schedule, then each year you only pay fees for one year, just like you would if you were waiting until payments were normally due. The upside is that then you can get the best reservations.

Know other key dates. Depending on your timeshare system and resort rules, there may be other key dates that affect when you should book your vacation. Knowing these dates is important for getting what you want. _Worksheet B - Using Your Timeshare_ gives you a convenient place to keep track of these details.

For example, if you own RCI Points (a hybrid weeks/points system), you'll have a schedule like this showing when you can make reservations:

▸ 13-months in advance for booking your home week (week you own)

▸ 12-months in advance for booking your home resort (other weeks)

▸ 11 months in advance for booking your home group

▸ 10-months in advance for other points reservations

Even if you're planning to book a week at your home resort, it's important to know the points deadlines, too. You can see from this schedule that your own resort will open up for any RCI points owner at the 10 month mark, which could mean an influx of new people wanting to reserve there. Booking before or after that 10-month deadline could make a big difference as far as getting the vacation you want.

Expert tip: How are "months in advance" calculated? Double check the rules. Some companies set deadlines based on months before check-in date, and others on months before check-out date. Some places open up reservations for a full week on a single day (i.e. check-ins on Thurs, Fri, Sat or Sun would all open for booking on Thursday). Still others have timing rules based around the dates the timeshare season starts or ends, rather than the dates of your specific visit. Find out how your timeshare works, and keep notes on your spreadsheet.

Want peak dates? Mark your calendar. Learn the rules for the resort where you want to stay. Figure out the specific dates you want to book, then work backward to calculate the key booking dates (12 months out, etc.) for your desired vacation. Mark those dates on your calendar, so that you know when you need to take action.

Super peak? May need to book within minutes. If you want to book a super high-demand vacation like New Year's Eve,

Mardi Gras, or the 4th of July, these peak slots can be hard to book, even when you're an owner at a resort. There are cases where you need to be online or on the phone within the first few minutes of the day reservations open up, or the dates you want could be gone.

Expert tip: Use check-in day to your advantage. Let's say your timeshare resort requires full-week stays to start on Fri, Sat or Sun. Your ideal schedule would be to stay starting on Sat, July 18. People who book the week starting on Fri, July 17 could get a head start on reservations though, so you might consider starting your request on Friday instead of Saturday.

What if you're not so particular? If your requirements aren't so specific, and you're not trying to book high demand dates, then you can be more relaxed in your planning. It still pays to make plans as early as you can, though. Options do dwindle as the year goes on, sometimes down to nothing.

Keep notes. Over time, you will learn how much lead time you need for booking certain types of vacations at your timeshare. This is valuable information for you. The worksheets included with this book give you a way to track this, so that a few years down the road, you'll remember what worked for you in the past.

In summary, planning further ahead works well in the world of timeshares, and you need to know the specific rules for your system and resort. Understanding your timeshare calendar and working the system accordingly is an important skill for getting the most value from your vacation ownership.

What happens if you wait?

The worst case scenario is that if you own a week, you could lose your entire vacation if you wait too long to do anything. This is an extreme case and doesn't happen often, but it is a possibility you surely want to avoid.

A more normal situation is that there are certain default actions that will happen if a deadline passes. Being aware of these helps you make the best use of your timeshare. Here are a few examples.

* With the **Hilton Grand Vacation Club**, you can book your week and season at your home resort from 9 to 12 months in advance. If you take no action, then after the 9-month mark, you get points and your vacation plans must be handled with points rather than with your week.

* **At many RCI Points resorts**, you can make a reservation for your week up to 12 months in advance. If you take no action at all, then when the 12-month mark passes, your week will be automatically deposited into RCI Points.

* **At other RCI Points resorts**, the 12-month date could come and go, and they wouldn't automatically deposit anything into RCI Points until you specifically request that they do this. If you take no action at these timeshares, your week is still there waiting for you to make a reservation.

As you can see, it's important to know the rules for your specific timeshare, so that you know what your options are, and how those options change as time goes by. It's a real shame to lose an opportunity just by waiting too long.

Another downside to waiting too long to make plans is that if you decide to make a trade, your exchange value declines. Read more about that in *Trading power and exchange value*.

Making a reservation

The procedures for making a reservation vary from place to place, so you'll need to find out how this works for your timeshare.

Online. Some companies have an automated booking system you can use. Make sure you've got your login details and password working, so you can use the system when you want. This is often the fastest and most convenient method, since you can make your travel plans 24 hours a day, and never need to wait on hold.

Phone. Many timeshares do not have an online system, and you need to call and make a reservation over the phone. The disadvantage to this is that you may have to spend more time and be limited to business hours. On the other hand, talking with a knowledgable person on the phone can give you a chance to ask questions or make a special request.

Expert tip: Note great contact people. If you find someone at your timeshare who is particularly helpful, make a note of their name and extension number, so you can speak with them again next time. Establishing a relationship with a great person can be very advantageous.

Mail. Some timeshares make you mail in a postcard at a certain time of year with your vacation choices. Fortunately, this is uncommon, and there is usually an easier way to do this.

Find out the details for your resort, and make a note of them. There is space to include this on *Worksheet B - Using Your*

Timeshare, so that you always have handy the login or contact details you need.

Getting the best unit on your vacation

If you own a fixed unit, then you know you will always get the same unit each time you use your timeshare. If you bought the 10th floor ocean view unit #1017, then that's what you'll get every time (as long you confirm it before any booking deadline).

Most timeshare owners do not have a fixed unit, however. It's more likely that you book a type of unit, rather than a specific numbered unit. When you book a generic 2-bedroom unit, you could end up with ocean view #1017, or parking lot view #206. Obviously your vacation will be enhanced if you have the balcony with the view, and wake to the sound of the waves every morning.

How can you optimize your chances of getting the unit you want?

Keep notes. When you visit a resort, you may discover that building C has the best views, the units by the pool are too noisy, or that #1402 is right by the elevator and ice machine. Keep notes of which locations you like or don't like, so that you can make requests in the future. If you travel to various places, it's very easy to forget these details, and notes can be a big help. *Worksheet B - Using Your Timeshare* has a section to record this information.

Expert tip: Use online reviews to find out about units. If you haven't visited a resort in person yet, check out the reviews on Tripadvisor.com. These often contain useful tidbits about which units are better than others.

Learn the rules. Different resorts have different rules about how they allocate units. Sometimes it's simply first come, first served - whoever checks in first that day, gets the first choice of units. Other places, there are specific guidelines. For example, a resort might have a rule that they only give the best view units to people who book a full 3-bedroom. If you split the 3-bedroom lock off into a 2-bedroom and a 1-bedroom, those smaller units won't be able to pull the best views.

See if they'll save it for you. It never hurts to ask. If you call in advance, some resorts will save you the unit you requested, or at least make a note in your file so the registration clerk can see your request. It doesn't always work, but when it does, it's wonderful. Try asking a month or more before you arrive, and see what they can do for you.

Give them a special reason. If you're asking for a prime unit, having a special occasion may make them more likely to honor your request. Is it your 10th wedding anniversary? A surprise trip for your spouse's 50th birthday? If there is a special reason, the resort staff will often be more inclined to give you a special unit.

Learn who's in charge, and schmooze. If you are a frequent visitor to a resort, it's useful to know a key individual there on a personal basis. Find out who knows the most about assigning rooms, or has the authority to influence those decisions. Introduce yourself, be friendly and nice, and establish a relationship with them. Often, this person will be the one who can best explain the rules to you, and describe the real difference between different units. Knowing the right person to talk to can go a long way.

Check again and reconfirm. Let's say you spoke with someone a month before your vacation, who said they'd put in a request for you to get that special unit you want. Call back a week before your trip, and see if the request is still there, still active, and likely to be honored. You might find that it's been lost in the shuffle, and can get it back on the books. Check again the day before you arrive, and try to talk to the front desk person who will be assigning the rooms. This way it will be fresh in that person's mind when you arrive.

Expert tip: Work the rules. If you can't get a special unit saved for you, can you work the rules? Let's say you know that the person who checks in first that day gets first choice on the units. All your flights to Hawaii get in late evening, and it looks like that will leave you without an ocean view. You could fly the night before, and stay somewhere else for one night, just so you are first in line to check in, and grab that ocean view unit. It's an extra expense, but is having that view for 7 nights worth the cost?

Send a thank you. If this is your home resort or a place you'll visit again in the future, it makes sense to build relationships. Be sure to thank the people at the resort who helped you get that primo unit you wanted. Let them know how much this meant to you, how grateful you are, and how wonderful it made your trip. This may mean they'll remember you, next year when you call.

Worksheet B - Using Your Timeshare

Summary

This worksheet covers the key information you need for using your own timeshare. This information doesn't change often, but it is a living document, in that you can continue adding information to this sheet as you learn more.

For instance, if you discover that you really like a particular set of units, or that a certain person is your best contact for special requests, you can note that information here for future reference. The next time you want to book a vacation with your timeshare, you will have that information handy.

How to use this worksheet

- **Timeshare basics** - This section has key high-level information about using your timeshare, such as whether it's annual or biennial, what weeks you can use it, check-in days allowed, or the dates for your points use year.

- **Making reservations** - Details on how to make reservations, such as the website URL and login, phone number and optional contact person, and how far in advance you can make reservations.

- **Deadlines to watch** - If there are key deadline dates, note those here. For instance, if you need to pool your points before the start date of your use year, that is a deadline to watch.

- **Timeline info** - This information is for your planning timeline. It includes your favorite time to visit, typical lead time required to book that, and when you need to start making reservations.

- **Getting the best units** - If you have found certain units that you particularly like or don't like, note that information here. You can also keep track of when and how to put in unit-specific requests.

- **Exchange options** - This is to note which exchange companies you can and have used for this timeshare.

Usage tips

- **Hard copy vs. online** - This works well as a hard copy printout that you keep in the front of your timeshare folder or binder. It does not change often, but every once in awhile, you will want to update it with new information and print out a new copy.

- **Multiple timeshares** - When you have multiple timeshares, just use a separate column on the sheet for each timeshare.

Links to worksheets

- SAMPLE worksheet - This copy is filled out with sample data for different types of timeshares. The data is not real - it's purely for illustration purposes, so you can see how the spreadsheet works.

- BLANK worksheet - For your own use.

- Worksheets are at *TimeshareGame.com/owners-guide-links/*

4. Option A1 - Using Your Week

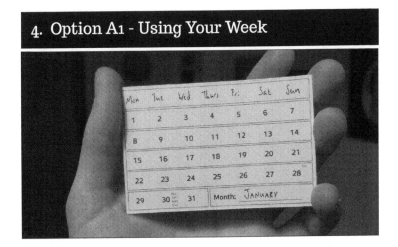

Timing concepts for using your week

Annual timeshares. Most timeshares are annual. When you own a timeshare week, that means you get one week to work with each year.

- **Activities can happen in different years**. Your schedule of activities will probably not line up with your allocated weeks. For example, you could make your 2016 reservation in 2015, or perhaps even 2014.

- **Vacationing in different years**. With your own week, you need to use it during the designated year. Once you move into exchanges, however, it's more complicated. For instance, you might decide to skip 2016 and take two trips in 2017 instead. We'll cover ways to do this in future chapters.

- **Plan around each underlying year**. The key point to remember is that you are allocated a week each year to be used one way or another. It is helpful to think in terms of this underlying year, to keep things straight.

  For instance, you're working with your 2016 week. You may end up making a reservation for this during 2015, or exchange it for a 2017 vacation, but it's still your 2016 week that you're working with.

Biennial timeshares. If you own a biennial timeshare, you own either Odd years or Even years. Even if you own an Odd year timeshare, you can end up with timeshare activities in even years, too. The key is to plan how you're going to use every year you get, and make sure you are not missing any opportunities. Triennial follows the same principle as biennial.

Getting the week you want

There are a couple of aspects to getting the timeshare dates you want at your home resort. First, it depends on what you own. Second, it depends on when you make your reservation.

What do you own? This is the single most important factor in determining what you can reserve at your home resort, and how you need to go about it. Here's a rundown, so you can see where your ownership fits.

Own a Fixed week. Your dates are fixed, as specified in your timeshare contract. This means that you have the right to book your own fixed week, in the specific unit type that you purchased. For instance, you might own a 2-BR unit for week 18, which falls in early May.

* **Do you want your week?** If so, then you're all set. Just notify the resort that you will be using the fixed week that you own.

  Watch out: Fixed weeks aren't always guaranteed. Even fixed weeks can disappear if you don't take a necessary action by a specific date. Some resorts auto-approve you for your fixed week. Others may require you to reserve your own unit 30 days in advance, or even 1 year + 1 day in advance. Make sure you know the rules at your resort, and get your reservation in at the right time.

* **Do you want something different?** What if you own week 18, but really want to use week 42 this year instead? Sometimes a resort will allow you to book a float week even if you own a fixed week, but that is resort dependent, and not a normal situation. Typically, your method to do this would be to trade your week through an exchange company, which means paying an exchange fee. You'll find a lot more about exchanges in *Option B - Exchanging Your Timeshare*.

Own a Floating week. In this case, you own a floating week in a specific season, for a certain type of unit. The resort has a chart of which weeks fall into the season you bought, and you have the right to book a vacation in your unit type during one of those weeks of the year.

- **Is this what you want?** If so, then you just need to make your reservation early enough, and you can get the week you want. Refer to the section *Make plans early*.

  Watch out: Float weeks can vanish. In a floating week system, some owners occasionally end up without any week to use. They have to pay their annual maintenance fees, but wind up without a vacation. The resort cannot sell more weeks than there are available, so how can this happen? Here's a scenario:

  ▸ Say you own a floating Silver timeshare you can use during weeks 14-21 (spring) and 43-50 (fall).

  ▸ The resort is totally sold out, so there are exactly the same number of owners as there are weeks available.

  ▸ Some owners book their fall weeks early in the year, while other owners wait to do anything.

  ▸ As the months go by, some of the units in spring weeks 14-21 end up sitting vacant because nobody reserved them.

  ▸ When it gets to week 38 and you decide you want to book something in the 43-50 range, it turns out that all of those fall weeks are taken! Every week that went unused in the spring means one owner who's left without anything.

  Note: Some resorts are proactive in managing unused weeks, and will deposit them into an exchange company. Then if you decide too late and the rest of your season is already taken, they could give you a week that was deposited for exchange. Not every resort does this, though, and it is far safer to stay on top of your own vacation planning.

Own a Hybrid week / points timeshare. In this type of system, you own a week that's also allocated a certain number of points. Depending on your timeshare system's rules, at some times, you may use it like a fixed or floating week. At other times you can use it like points.

For example, if you are an owner in the Bluegreen Vacation Club, you might own a deeded fixed week 33 that also gives you 20,000 points. If you book 13 months in advance, you can reserve your own fixed week. If you wait until 11 months in advance, your fixed week is open for others to book, and you use your points instead. Booking with points is covered in _Option A2 - Using Your Points_.

Chart - Weeks in different timeshare systems

The chart below gives an overview of how booking your timeshare week works in some of the most popular timeshare systems in the US.

Company	How it works
Bluegreen Vacation Club (BVC)	You can reserve your deeded week up to 13 months in advance. At 11 months out, your week is converted to points that are deposited in your account.
Diamond Resorts International (DRI)	If you own a deeded week, the rules on using it can vary by resort.
Disney Vacation Club (DVC)	No weeks ownership, all points.
Hilton Grand Vacation Club (HGVC)	You can reserve your home week up to 12 months in advance. At 9 months out, it switches to points and you use points for reservations after that.

Company	How it works
Marriott Vacation Club (MVC)	If you own a week, you can usually reserve it 12 months in advance. Multiple week owners can sometimes book up to 13 months in advance.
RCI Points	You can reserve your home week up to 13 months in advance. Usually at 12 months out it will automatically be deposited into points instead.
Starwood Vacation Ownership (SVO)	You can reserve your deeded week up to 12 months in advance.
Vacation Resorts International (VRI)	Rules for using your timeshare week vary by resort. Some resorts allow booking up to 2 years in advance.
Westgate Resorts	You can reserve your week up to 11 months in advance.
Worldmark, The Club	No weeks ownership, all points.
Wyndham (Club Wyndham)	Reservations are handled as points, even if you have an underlying deeded week.

As you can see, the rules vary quite a bit between timeshare systems, and sometimes even for different owners in the same system. It is important for you to verify your own timeshare's rules. _Worksheet B - Using Your Timeshare_ gives you a handy place to document the rules and dates for your timeshare.

Process overview for using your week

Here's a general approach for using your own timeshare week. The specifics will vary depending on your timeshare, but this is the basic process.

This is covered in detail in _Creating Your Timeshare Calendar_, along with how to put all of your timeshare activities together into a coordinated plan.

☑   Decide on the dates you want.

☑   Determine the lead time you need for a reservation.

☑   Set up a reminder for when the reservation needs to be made.

☑   Make your reservations on the date you determined.

We've talked a lot about planning in advance, and booking vacations a year or more beforehand. To make the best use of the timeshare you own, planning in advance really does yield the best results.

Does this mean you can't be spontaneous when you own a timeshare, and take off for a last minute getaway? Of course not. It is often easy to get shoulder season or off season bookings without much lead time. In addition, you'll find some other options for spur of the moment vacations in the section _Traveling on short notice_.

5. Option A2 - Using Your Points

Timing concepts for using your points

In a points system, rather than owning a week at a specific resort, you have a pool of points that you can spend as you choose (within the constraints of your system).

It's kind of like timeshare money. You spend your real money (cold hard cash) when you buy your timeshare and pay the annual fees. This gives you the timeshare money (points) that you use for your vacations.

Annual points. Most points-based timeshares are annual, which means that every 12 months, you get a designated number of points that you can use. Your annual cycle may start on January 1 or some other date.

Expiration dates. Your points always have an expiration date, and you need to take some action with them before then. You have other options besides booking a vacation (more on that later), but you need to do something or they will expire and you get nothing.

Activities can happen in different years. You will have activities related to your points that happen in other years. For instance, you could book your 2017 points vacation during 2016.

Points offer timing flexibility. Depending on what timeshare system you are in, you may have options that let you borrow points from future years, or extend current points to last longer.

Plan around your use years. You are allocated points each year to be used one way or another. You may have points from multiple years in your account at the same time, with different expiration dates. It is helps keep things straight to think of your points in terms of which use year they're from, and track them this way.

Biennial timeshare. If you own a biennial (every other year, or EOY)timeshare, you own either Odd years or Even years, but you will still have timeshare activities in the other years, too. You could make a 2016 reservation during 2015, spend some points in 2016, and roll some forward to 2017.

Expert tip: Biennial rules can be complicated. Some points systems are complex for a biennial timeshare. If you own something like this, it is especially important to track which points are which. For example, if you own a Biennial Odd years 10,000 point timeshare with the Bluegreen Vacation Club, here's how it would work.

▸ Points are only added to your account during Odd years, but they aren't all the same kind of points.

▸ 2015 - You get your points. You get 5,000 "annual" points (2015) in your account + 5,000 "borrowed" points (2016).

▸ 2016 - If you didn't use any points yet, your 5,000 "annual" 2015 points are now treated as "saved" for 2016, and have some usage restrictions. Your 5,000 "borrowed" 2016 points are now available for normal use.

Triennial. This is the same principle as biennial. Even though you only get points every third year, you will have timeshare activities in other years, too.

Hybrid weeks/points systems. If you own a timeshare in a hybrid system (for example RCI Points), then sometimes you can use it as a week, and other times you can use it as points. This section is all about the points. For more on how to use your week, see *Option A1 - Using Your Week*.

Anniversaries and use years

What is a use year? In an annual system (the simplest), your points are allocated to you every use year. These are typically tied to your anniversary with the timeshare company, and may not match the calendar year. For instance, you may have a use year that runs from April 1 to March 31.

The idea is that you're supposed to use those points for a vacation during that use year. There are ways around this (see *Working with points*), but the normal situation is that you use your points during their assigned use year.

Expert tip: Tracking multiple use years. If you own more than one timeshare, you can easily end up with different anniversaries and use years. For instance, you could have one points timeshare that starts on April 1 every year, and another that starts July 1. This makes keeping track of your points, use years, expiration dates, and timeshare activities even more important so you don't miss anything.

When do you get your points? Depending on what timeshare system you own, this can vary. Here are some possible scenarios.

- **Start of use year**. You get the points deposited in your account on the first day of your use year. If your year runs from April 1 to March 31, you'd get all of your points on April 1 each year.

- **Prior to use year**. You get the points earlier than your use year. For instance, you could get your points on March 1 even though your year doesn't start until April 1, to facilitate making reservations earlier than 12 months out.

- **Based on action with week**. This can happen with a hybrid timeshare. For example, you could have the right to reserve your week from 12 to 13 months in advance. If you don't take the week, you get your points at the 12 month mark.

- **When you request them**. Some resorts won't deposit your timeshare week into points until you make a specific request to do so.

- **Borrowing from the future**. You may have an option to "borrow" points from future years. You can find more on that in *Working with points*.

When do you lose your points? All of the points you get have an expiration date. There are ways you can extend this, but if you don't do something with your points before the expiration date, you will lose them. You will pay your annual fee and get no benefit. Don't let that happen!

Expert tip: Vacations near beginning vs. end of use year. Say your use year runs from July 1 to June 30 each year. If you book a May vacation, then have to cancel for some reason, you have little time left in your use year, with points slated to expire June 30. If you book a July vacation, then have to change your plans, those points are still good for many months. Note that cancellation rules vary in different timeshares.

Full weeks vs. short stays

One thing many people like about a points-based timeshare compared to owning a week is that you can take shorter vacations. You're not tied to vacationing in 7-night chunks.

You can decide to take 2 nights here, 4 nights there, or 12 nights somewhere else.

Book weekend getaways. When work and school schedules allow only limited vacation time, it's nice to be able to take short getaways now and then. With a points-based timeshare, you can do this whenever you want. If weekend trips work best for you, you can use all of your points on weekend stays.

Split your week of vacation. If you have a week to spend on vacation, you don't need to spend the entire week in one place. You could split it and spend 3 nights at one resort, and 4 nights at another.

Get more with mid-week stays. Demand is always higher on weekends, which means that those nights require the most points. When you get a full week, you pay for both a weekend and the attached week nights. If your schedule allows mid-week travel, you can use points to book just the mid-week nights. Since these have lower points costs, this approach can give you more total vacation nights than getting a full week or booking weekends.

Short stays can mean more fees. The downside of booking short stays is that you can incur higher fees. It makes sense in a way, because short stays mean more work for reservations and check-in staff. Details will depend on your system, but here's an example from RCI Points.

▸ 7-night stay, transaction fee = $169

▸ 4-night stay, transaction fee = $109

▸ 3 night stay, transaction fee = $89

▸ Split week 3-nights + 4 nights, fee = $198 vs. Full week fee of $169

How many points does it cost?

Using your timeshare points is a matter of looking at what's available, and seeing what you can get with your points. The points chart for your timeshare system is the key document that tells you how much it costs to book different things.

Let's say that you own points in the Wyndham system, and you're thinking of visiting Sedona, Arizona to explore the red rock country. Here is a condensed version of the points chart for the Wyndham Sedona, with a few notes.

Season	Wks	Day/Wk	1BR-B	1BR-A	2BR
Value	2-4 50-51	Sun-Thur	9,000	10,500	18,000
		Fri-Sat	19,500	21,000	32,000
		Full week	84,000	94,500	154,000
High	5-10 48-49	Sun-Thur	12,000	13,000	21,000
		Fri-Sat	22,500	23,500	35,000
		Full week	105,000	112,000	175,000
Prime	1, 52 11-47	Sun-Thur	15,000	17,000	22,600
		Fri-Sat	25,500	27,500	38,000
		Full week	126,000	140,000	189,000

Season definitions. There are different prices for Value, High and Prime season. Looking at the Weeks column shows you that Value season (the cheapest) is restricted to late December and January. High season (the middle) includes February, early March, and early December. The rest of the year is classified as Prime (the most expensive).

Different unit types. You can see on the chart that you can get a 2-bedroom unit or two kinds of 1-bedroom. There are separate notes that explain the difference:

▸ The more expensive 1BR-A has a full kitchen, whirlpool tub, balcony, and 974 square feet.

▸ The less expensive 1BR-B has a mini kitchen, no whirlpool tub or balcony, and 558 square feet.

Usage restrictions. There are footnotes on the chart that spell out certain restrictions on your use. While points allow a great deal of flexibility, you can't always book exactly what you want. Here are the rules for this resort:

▸ Full week stays require check-in on Fri, Sat, or Sun.

▸ 3 or 4 night stays in Prime season require check-in OR check-out on Fri, Sat, or Sun.

What could you do? Scenarios. Let's say that you own 112,000 points - enough to book a full week in the larger 1-bedroom during the High season. Here are a few scenarios for how you could work this.

▸ **Full week** in large 1BR (with balcony and full kitchen) in February.
(7 nights total)

▸ **2-BR long weekend** (3 nights including Fri+Sat) in September.
(3 nights total)

▸ **Two weekend getaways** in May and Oct (large 1BR, Fri +Sat stays).
(4 nights total)

▸ **Three 4-night stays** in a small 1BR, January, no weekends.
(12 nights total)

Weighing your options. As you can see, there are a lot of different ways to use your points. Depending on your group size, schedule restrictions and travel preferences, 112,000 points could get you anywhere from 3 to 12 nights in Sedona. Throw in the fact that you've got a lot of other resorts you could visit too, and you've got enough options to keep you thinking for awhile!

Getting the dates you want

Just because you've got enough points to book a specific vacation doesn't mean that it will be available. Popular resorts, peak seasons, and weekends can fill up quickly.

As discussed in _Make plans early_, the more lead time you allow in your vacation planning, the better your chances of getting what you want. Here are a few other tips for getting what you want with your points.

Have options for dates or resorts. Let's say you have points in the Wyndham system mentioned above, and you want to do a family vacation to Durango, Colorado in July. That's peak season, and a lot of people like to visit then. The more flexible you can be, the more likely you are to get what you want.

▸ Dates - Work with a range of dates, rather than one specific week.

▸ Resorts - Consider alternate resorts like Pagosa Springs or Steamboat Springs if you have trouble booking Durango.

Know the rules and plan your dates. How far in advance are you allowed to make a reservation? This is a key fact you need to know for your timeshare system. If you're trying to book a high-demand time slot, you'll want to make that reservation as early as possible.

For example, you could book the Wyndham Durango starting 10 months before the check-in date. If you want a vacation starting July 18, 2016, you could make that reservation starting Sept 18, 2015. The closer to that date that you make your booking, the better your chances.

Expert tip: Longer stays can get you priority. If your system calculates reservation dates based on check-in date, then people who book longer stays that start earlier can get an advantage. For example, say you want to book a ski trip over President's Day weekend, and that's a hard reservation to get. Can you take a longer vacation that starts earlier? If you can start your vacation a few days sooner, you could get booking priority over people trying to make that high demand reservation starting that Friday.

Holidays and special events are tough. Holidays like the 4th of July, or special events like Daytona bike week, can make reservations very difficult to get. If you want to book something like that, you need to move fast and make your booking as soon as you can. Sometimes these can fill up within minutes.

Priority booking at your home resort. Many hybrid weeks/ points timeshare systems give owners an advanced booking window for vacations at their home resort, so they can get a jump on everyone else who wants to stay there. If that's where you want to vacation, then make use of this priority booking period.

Chart - Using points in different systems

Here's a chart showing the basic rules for reservation times in some of the most popular timeshare systems in the US. You can use this as a starting point for planning. If you own a hybrid weeks/points timeshare, also check the *Chart - Weeks in different timeshare systems*, since you may be able to use your timeshare both ways.

Company	How it works
Bluegreen Vacation Club (BVC)	You can book your points reservation up to 11 months in advance.
Diamond Resorts International (DRI)	For DRI collection/trust based points, you can book in your "home club" 13 months out. For DRI week-based points, you can book your "home resort" 12 months out. Other reservations are up to 10 months prior.
Disney Vacation Club (DVC)	You can book at your home resort up to 11 months out, and up to 7 months in advance elsewhere.
Hilton Grand Vacation Club (HGVC)	You can book an HGVC vacation with your points up to 9 months in advance.
Marriott Vacation Club (MVC)	It's a bit complicated, but generally Premiere members can book 13 months in advance, all members can book a 7+ night stay 12 months in advance, and all members can book stays < 7 nights 10 months ahead.
RCI Points	For RCI Points resorts, you can book your home resort up to 12 months out, your home group up to 11 months out, and everywhere else up to 10 months out. You can also book an RCI Weeks resort up to 24 months in advance.
Starwood Vacation Ownership (SVO)	If your timeshare gets Staroption points, you can use them within the Starwood network up to 8 months in advance.

Company	How it works
Vacation Resorts International (VRI)	There are no VRI points. Some VRI weeks may be part of RCI Points.
Westgate Resorts	Westgate is weeks only.
Worldmark, The Club	You can reserve with a 7-night minimum up to 13 months in advance. Red season stays <7 nights can only be booked 9 months prior.
Wyndham (Club Wyndham)	You can book your home resort up to 13 months in advance. Other reservations can be made up to 10 months in advance.

Working with points

One thing about using a timeshare system like this is that the number of points you use for vacations will often not be exactly the same as the number of points you have in your account. You may have almost (but not quite) enough points to get what you want, or you may end up with points left over.

As discussed in _Anniversaries and Use Years_, your points will be assigned to a particular use year, and each group of points will have a certain expiration date. So what happens when your numbers don't quite match?

Most timeshare systems give you some flexible options for working with your points. Specifics and terminology depend on your system, but here are some common things to do with your points.

Borrow from a future year. If you don't have enough points for the vacation you want, you can borrow from a future year's allocation of points.

Rent extra points. This is another way to get some extra points - you just rent a one-time usage of points. You may be able to rent points from the timeshare company or another owner.

Save or extend points. This is a way to increase the life of your points by extending the expiration date. There may be limits, such as a maximum 3-year life for any points.

Transfer points. You can often transfer some of your unused points to another owner in the same timeshare system, or they can transfer points to you. If there's an exchange of money for this, then it's basically the same as one owner renting points to another. In some systems, it's OK to give the points away but not to do it for money, so check your rules.

As you might expect, there are fees associated with these different points transactions, too. As you might also expect, fees tend to go up over time.

Specifics on how to do these things vary by company, so you need to verify the rules for your own timeshare system. Make sure to note date limitations on when you can exercise your options. For instance, if you want to save some points for a future year, when do you need to take action on that?

Expert tip: Learn the rules, then keep them handy. _Worksheet A - Timeshare Info Sheet_ gives you a place to note the rules that apply for your points, so that you have all the information you need in one place, and don't need to go research it again when you have a question.

Process overview for using your points

Here's a general approach for using your timeshare points. The specifics will vary depending on your timeshare, but this is the basic process. This is covered in detail in _Creating Your_

Timeshare Calendar, along with how to put all your timeshare activities together into a coordinated plan.

☑ Find a resort where you'd like to stay.

☑ Evaluate what you can get with your points, and see what works best.

☑ Decide on the dates you want, and determine the lead time you need.

☑ Set up a reminder for when the reservation needs to be made.

☑ Make your reservations on the date you determined.

☑ Use leftover points for last-minute getaways, when possible.

Worksheet C - Tracking Points

Summary

Staying on top of your points is essential to making the most of your timeshare, and it can get complicated. This worksheet helps you track the points you have received and what you did with them. The goal is to manage your points effectively, so that you always know at a glance what you have, and never let anything expire unused. You can also easily see how you used your points in the past, to help you remember what worked well.

The worksheet shows your vacations reserved and completed, points saved to the next year, and points borrowed from future years. It also highlights what points you currently have available, and what their expiration dates are.

How to use this worksheet

- **Sections by use year** - Down the left side of the spreadsheet are sections of rows for each use year. These cover the points that you received for that use year, as well as what you did with them. Note that your use year may not correspond to the calendar year.

- **Points received** - At the start of each use year is a row showing the points you receive deposited in your account. Points received are entered with their expiration date.

- **Vacations booked and taken** - Whenever you book a vacation, enter the details here, such as the location, date, and unit type. Subtract the points used from your total available. Pending vacations (booked but not taken yet) are color coded so you can easily see what trips you have coming up.
  Note: If you use your points for other purposes, such as a hotel stay or car rental, just enter it the same way you would for booking a vacation with your points, so you can track all points expenditures together.

- **Saving points** - When you save some or all of your points for a future year, there are entries to close out those points from one year, and add them to the next, with a new expiration date. For instance, if you had 10,360 points from 2015 that you saved for 2016, you would subtract those points from 2015 and add them to 2016 with the new expiration date.

- **Borrowing points** - When you borrow points from a future year, you subtract them from that year, and add them to the year you're using them. For example, if you borrow 43,640 points from 2017 to use in 2016, you would subtract them from 2017 and add them to 2016.

- **Transferring or renting points** - If you transfer your points to someone else, just subtract there here, and make an appropriate note about what happened. If you rent points to augment your own set, then add them here, once again with a comment about what happened.

- **Open points** - Open points are those which are currently available for your use. These are highlighted in yellow, since these are the points that are most important for you to pay attention to right now. Always be sure to do something with these points before they expire.

- **Weeks used** - In some systems, you have the option to use your week rather than taking the points. In this case, you would show the week as a vacation booked, with a notation about why there were no points received that year.

- **Transaction fees** - When you pay a fee for booking a vacation, or saving or borrowing points, this is where you can note how much the fee was and the date that you paid it.

- **Dates to watch** - If you have certain dates coming up that you need to pay attention to, highlight those on this sheet. For instance, your open points have an expiration date to watch, or you could have a deadline to pool or extend your points.

Usage tips

- **Multiple timeshares, same system** - If you own more than one timeshare in the same system, track them together on a single worksheet. For instance, you could have more than one timeshare in RCI points. Keep them together on the same sheet, so that you can see all of your RCI points in one place.

- **Multiple types of points** - If you own more than one type of points, add another tab to the Excel workbook so that you have a separate worksheet for each. For example, you might have a tab for RCI points and another for Wyndham points. These are two totally different types of points, so you need to track them separately.

- **This is a living document** - Since this document will be changing every time you receive new points, use your points for a vacation, or work with points by renting, borrowing or saving, it's easiest to keep this document on your computer. Printed copies get out of date quickly.

Expert tip: Review this worksheet regularly.
Check this frequently, and keep it up to date. If you
don't pay attention to what you have and your
critical dates, you may end up losing some points, or
not making the best use of them. Set up a schedule for
checking your points, and make sure that you're always on top
of what's happening.

Links to worksheets

● SAMPLE worksheet - This copy is filled out with sample
data for different types of timeshares. The data is not real
- it's purely for illustration purposes, so you can see how
the spreadsheet works.

● BLANK worksheet - For your own use.

● Worksheets are at
TimeshareGame.com/owners-guide-links/

6. Option B - Exchanging Your Timeshare

As much as you enjoy vacationing using your own timeshare, there will be times when you want to go somewhere else instead. This is where timeshare exchanges come in.

You can exchange the timeshare you own for a vacation at thousands of resorts around the world. You aren't tied to your own resort, season, or timeshare company. The ability to exchange what you own for a vacation elsewhere is a key benefit of owning a timeshare, since it gives you tremendous flexibility and a multitude of options.

How the exchange happens will be different based on whether you own weeks vs. points, what timeshare system you are part of, and what avenue you use to handle the exchange. This section discusses the different approaches you can take to exchanging your timeshare.

Different timeshare exchange methods

There are various avenues you can use to exchange your timeshare to vacation somewhere else. Here's a quick overview. Subsequent sections will delve deeper into different methods.

Exchange in your own company system. Depending on what timeshare company you own with, you may want to exchange your timeshare through their company system. This may be handled as a week-for-week exchange, or via points.

For instance, if you own a week with Westgate, you can trade through their company exchange system to spend a week at a different Westgate resort. If you own a week with Hilton, then you can use the associated points to book a stay at a different Hilton resort. The section _Exchanging through your company system_ provides more information.

Private exchange between individuals. This is the simplest method conceptually, and can be effective when it works. You own timeshare A, somebody else owns timeshare B, and you set up a private exchange, handled strictly between the two of you. The only problem is that it can be hard to find someone who's a good match for a trade. You can find more information in _Direct exchange with another owner_.

Major exchange companies. There are two major exchange companies that have networks of thousands of resorts. These are **RCI** and **Interval International (II)**. Almost every timeshare worldwide is associated with one of these two exchange companies, and some are dual-affiliated with both. Sections _Option B1 - Exchanging with RCI_ and _Option B2 - Exchanging with Interval_ have all the details on using these systems.

The way it works is that rather than finding a trade on your own, you deposit your timeshare with the exchange company. Thousands of other timeshare owners do the same. You can search to see what other people have made available, and grab the exchange you want.

Independent exchange companies. To use one of the major exchange companies, your timeshare resort has to be affiliated with them. There are also a number of smaller, independent timeshare exchange companies. These aren't tied to specific resorts like RCI or II are, and are open to owners with many different companies.

There are pros and cons to consider about using one of the smaller exchange companies instead of the big two. See _Using an independent exchange company_ for more on this approach.

Rent yours out and rent another. This isn't technically an exchange, but it's a method some people use quite successfully to accomplish the same goal. The idea with this is that you rent out your timeshare to a third party, then use the cash you get to rent a different timeshare vacation for yourself from somebody else.

The advantages of this system are its flexibility (you aren't tied to any company's rules, schedule, or availability), and the fact that you're not paying exchange company fees. On the other hand, there is some work involved with renting out your timeshare. For more on this approach, look at the sections *Renting out your timeshare* and *Renting someone else's timeshare*.

Overview of the exchange process

What normally happens when you want to do an exchange is that you deposit your timeshare into the exchange system you're going to use. When you do this, it becomes part of the inventory they make available to other people. If you deposit your California timeshare, this will become available for people who want to trade into California. If you're hoping to exchange that for Hawaii, then you're looking for other people to deposit their Hawaii timeshares, so you can get those on exchange.

The exchange companies handle thousands of resorts and have many, many listings available. The large number of people participating gives you a good selection of possibilities, and their online systems facilitate the exchange process.

Availability considerations. The perfect timeshare exchange you're hoping to find won't always be available. Remember that owners generally have first choice on using their own units or reserving in their own points system. If you're hoping to get a peak week at a prime resort, like Christmas week at a slope-side ski resort, it can be rare to see it available for exchange. The supply is limited, and owners often want to use those peak time periods themselves.

Flexibility makes it easier. If you're flexible in what you're looking for, you'll have more success with exchanges. If you want a week somewhere at Lake Tahoe any time during the kids' summer vacation, that's far more likely than if you only want July 7-13, at one specific resort. Being flexible gives you a better chance of finding something to fit your needs.

Deposit first vs. Request first. The normal scenario described above is "Deposit first," where you deposit your timeshare first, then make your exchange. Some companies also allow "Request first," where you first put in your request for the exchange you want. When a match comes through for you, then you deposit your timeshare at that point. There are pros and cons to each approach, which are discussed more in later sections.

Depositing your timeshare

When you deposit your timeshare (also called banking it), you give your timeshare to the exchange company, and it goes into their pool of properties available for exchange. Other people do the same thing. You can then choose a vacation you want from that pool, and complete the trade.

You can't get it back. Once your week is deposited with an exchange company, it's theirs to offer to other people. You can't change your mind and get it back. If you decide that you really want to stay at your home resort after all, you would need to do it as an exchange back to your resort. This would cost you a fee, like any other exchange.

No using your timeshare anymore. Once you deposit your week with an exchange company, it belongs to them and they make it available to other people for exchanges. You no longer have the right to use it yourself, rent it out to someone else, or arrange a direct owner to owner exchange. It is no longer your timeshare.

Depositing a fixed week. If you own a fixed week, then you know in advance what week you own, and it's the same every year. You don't have a choice about what week you deposit.

Depositing a floating week. If you own a floating week, you need to go through your resort to handle the deposit, since they need to confirm what week you get. Most places, you can request what week you want deposited, for instance, the week starting Oct. 14. Other resorts give you little ability to determine the week that is deposited - they make that decision for you.

When to deposit? Deposit early. The general rule of thumb with the major exchange companies is that the closer it gets to the check-in date, the lower the trading power you get for your deposit. It's like losing money.

Maintenance fees. In order to deposit your week, you normally have to pay your maintenance fees first. This may mean that to get the most trading power, you need to pay your fees before their due date. For instance, if you have a May week and fees are normally due January 1, waiting to pay on the due date will only let you deposit your week 4 months in advance. You won't get the maximum trade value this way.

Paying estimated fees early. If you want to get a head start on this rather than waiting for your yearly maintenance bill, call your resort and request to pay early so you can get your week deposited. The way this normally works is that they will give you an estimated amount to pay at this time. When the normal due date rolls around, you may get another bill for any difference between the estimated fees you paid and the final fees due.

Like to Like exchanges

A basic concept in many timeshare exchanges is trading "Like for Like." The idea is that you can't expect to trade your timeshare for something much more valuable, like exchanging an off-season studio for a high season 2-bedroom. There are a couple of aspects to this "like for like" comparison.

Unit size. If you have a 1-bedroom, a straight "like for like" exchange would be to another 1-bedroom.

Season. If you have a High season timeshare, you could exchange for another High season unit somewhere else. If you own a Low season timeshare, you'd get another Low season. Note that the season definitions vary by resort, so February could be high season one place and low season somewhere else.

Put it together, and it means that with a "Like for Like" exchange, you would be trading your off-season studio for a different off-season studio somewhere else.

Different timeshare exchange companies have incorporated this concept in different ways, and have their own methods for how to get around it.

Upgrading and downgrading

There are obvious limitations to the strict "like for like" scenario. Sometimes you really want to travel in a different season than what you own, or you may want a larger unit for a family vacation. So how can you arrange an exchange like this? Here are a few ways that companies handle this.

Upgrade with an additional fee. With some of the smaller exchange companies you can get an upgraded timeshare on your trade if you pay a fee. This could mean a larger unit or better dates. For instance, with Dial an Exchange, there is an upgrade fee of $75 for each room size you move up.

Upgrade with more points / trading power. In a points system, the upgrade concept is easily handled by charging more points for larger units and higher demand seasons. If you want to upgrade from what you own, you can do this with more points (saved, borrowed, or rented). RCI uses a similar concept for timeshare weeks, called trading power. This is explained in detail in _Option B1 - Exchanging with RCI_.

Upgrade on shorter notice. In Interval International, you cannot put in an exchange request for a unit larger than the one you are trading, but as your check-in date gets closer, you can sometimes see larger units available. In practical terms, this means it's hard to book an upgrade far in the future, but they may be available for short notice bookings. This is covered in *Option B2 - Exchanging with Interval*.

The methods above give you ways to upgrade your exchange when you want to, but what about when you get a lower-value exchange? If some of the 3-bedroom timeshares deposited for exchange are given to owners of smaller units as upgrades, then there will be some 3-bedroom owners who are unable to get a unit as large as they own. These people will end up with a downgrade on their exchange. What happens then?

Downgrade and save points / trading power. Just like points systems can easily handle upgrades, they handle downgrades simply, too. A smaller unit or lower demand season will cost less points, and leave you with points left over to use elsewhere. Once again, the RCI Weeks trading power concept is similar.

Downgrade and get a bonus. With Interval International, if you end up taking an exchange that's a smaller unit or clearly of less value, then you may get a bonus week for your exchange. Bonus weeks are usually limited to places with ample timeshare availability, but it's still nice to get something.

Downgrade and get nothing extra. Some companies have no provision for anything special, and if you end up getting a downgrade on your exchange, that's simply the price of going where you want to go. Just figure this in your calculations when you're deciding whether to take that exchange or not. If you really want a 1-bedroom on the beach, then trading your 2-bedroom somewhere else may be well worth it, even if technically it's a downgrade.

Trading power and exchange value

A more sophisticated approach to timeshare trading than "like for like" is to assign each timeshare a certain trading power or exchange value based on a number of factors.

▸ Popularity of the destination

▸ Supply and demand for the resort

▸ Resort quality, facilities, and amenities

▸ Unit size and type

▸ Timeshare season and holiday schedule

▸ How far in advance you deposit your timeshare

Based on these criteria, the timeshare you own is assigned a certain amount of trading power. The exchange company keeps track of what each timeshare in their system is worth. The timeshares you can exchange into will depend on the relative value (trading power) of the timeshare you deposit vs. the one you want to book.

The trading power of your timeshare can vary over time. The general rule is that you get more trading power when you deposit your timeshare with the exchange company further in advance. This makes sense, because it gives more people a chance to request it. If you deposit your timeshare just a month before the check-in date, you will get little trade value for it, because most people already have their vacation plans set, and only short-notice travelers will be able to use it.

Trading power may be visible or invisible. In RCI, you can see the trading power that is assigned to each of your timeshare deposits. In Interval International, they have their own calculation for this but it's hidden away behind the scenes.

Expert tip: Trading power calculations vary between systems. Different systems assign more or less importance to the factors in calculating trading power. For instance, you may find that in one system, a 1-bedroom is valued much more highly than a studio, while another system gives little difference between them. This could mean that the studio does better trading in one system, while the 1-bedroom does better in the other.

Expert tip: Short notice can yield great trades. One time the regular trading power considerations don't carry as much weight is on short notice exchanges. Sometimes last minute cancellations create great trade opportunities but you've got to be able to jump on them when they appear. You may see a terrific opportunity show up, and two minutes later it will be gone.

Exchanging through your company system

Most timeshares are part of a group of associated resorts run by the same developer or management company. One of the benefits of buying into a group of properties is that you get certain rights when it comes to vacationing within this company network.

Just like most things in the timeshare world, the specifics depend on which company you are part of, as each one has their own rules. Here are some ways this can work, and benefits you may see.

Booking with points. In points systems, if you want to reserve a vacation at any of the resorts in your company network, you generally just book it with your points. You don't need to deposit your timeshare or go through any exchange company.

Internal exchanges. With some companies, if you want to stay at a different property within the developer's network of resorts, you can do an internal exchange. This doesn't go through the major exchange companies (RCI or Interval), and you typically pay a lower fee than you would to exchange through an external company.

Discount exchanges. In other cases, if you want to exchange for another resort in the same company, you still go through an outside exchange like Interval International, but you pay a lower price to exchange to a resort in your company network than you would to exchange elsewhere.

Preferential exchanges. Some timeshare owners have to go through a major exchange company, but get a preferential exchange when trading into their own company's resorts. For instance, if you own a Starwood week, you can exchange it in II, with preferential rights for booking other Starwood properties. Starwood owners get first crack at Starwood weeks deposited, before they open up for other exchangers.

Weeks and points in the same system. Some timeshare companies have a combination of weeks owners, points owners, and hybrid weeks/points owners, and the way the system works is different depending upon which group you are in. Make sure to verify the rules for the type of ownership you have.

Expert tip: Can't use the points system? If you own a week with a company that now does points, don't fret. A salesperson is bound to want you to "upgrade" to the points system, but don't feel that you need to do that. Even if they don't let you book with points inside their network, you can still trade your week for thousands of other possibilities. Before you make any changes, read *Owner's update = More high pressure sales*.

Restrictions on resale units. Some companies restrict aspects of your membership if you buy a resale timeshare rather than buying at full retail price directly from the developer. If that's what you own, in almost every case, you can still use the major exchange companies to travel all over. The money you saved on the purchase price can cover a lot of exchange fees!

Learn more: Resale restrictions cut both ways. Companies put resale restrictions in place to make their retail timeshares more attractive. However, even if you pay the full retail price and buy from the developer, this can work against you. Learn more about how this works in *Resale limitations - a double edged sword*, at *TimeshareGame.com/owners-guide-links/*

Watch out: Rules can change. Companies usually give themselves the right to change the rules when they want to. For example, one timeshare company changed their internal exchange system so that owners of resale timeshares are charged a $450 exchange fee - far more than people who bought straight from the developer. It doesn't make any sense to pay such an exorbitant fee when you can go through an exchange company instead, and get more choices for lower fees.

The following chart gives an overview of how an exchange within the company system works for some of the most popular timeshare companies in the United States. Note that there can be variations even within the same company based on the specific ownership you have (weeks, points, resale, etc.).

Company	How it works
Bluegreen Vacation Club (BVC)	Use your points to book within the Bluegreen system.
Diamond Resorts International (DRI)	Owners with DRI points can book resorts in this system with their points. Owners with pure weeks (no points) must go through an exchange company.

Company	How it works
Disney Vacation Club (DVC)	Use your points to book within the Disney system.
Hilton Grand Vacation Club (HGVC)	Use your points to book within the Hilton system.
Marriott Vacation Club (MVC)	Owners with Marriott Destination Club points can book resorts in the system with their points. Owners with pure weeks get preferential trades through Interval International.
RCI Points	Use your points to book at an RCI resort.
Starwood Vacation Ownership (SVO)	Owners with Staroption points can use them within the Starwood network. Other owners get preferential trades through Interval International.
Vacation Resorts International (VRI)	Exchange your week through the VRI*ety exchange network.
Westgate Resorts	Exchange your week through Westgate's internal exchange system.
Worldmark, The Club	Use your points to book within the Worldmark system.
Wyndham (Club Wyndham)	Use your points to book within the Wyndham system.

Find out the specific rules for the timeshare you own, so you know what exchanges are available to you, at what cost. You can then make educated decisions about when to exchange within your company system vs. going outside through a timeshare exchange company.

Using the major exchange companies

Company systems may have dozens or even hundreds of properties, but they're still limited compared to the number of timeshare resorts out there in the world. If you want to expand your choices, you can go through one of the major exchange companies. This gives you a larger set of resorts to choose from. With over 5,000 timeshare resorts around the world, you could stay in a different resort every week for the rest of your life.

You pay an annual membership fee to join an exchange company, and this gives you access to their collection of resorts. You also pay fees when you make exchanges, as well as for certain other transactions.

The major timeshare exchange companies are:

RCI (Resort Condominiums International). This is the largest timeshare network, with over 4,000 resorts for you to choose from, in almost 100 countries around the world.

Interval International (II). This is the second largest timeshare network, with about 2,700 different resorts in 75 countries.

Here are some considerations about using the major exchange companies.

Your timeshare must be affiliated. Which of these companies you can use depends on which of these networks your resort is affiliated with. If you buy a timeshare that's affiliated with RCI, then you can use RCI. To use Interval International, your timeshare needs to be associated with II. Most timeshares belong to one system or the other, so your options are fixed.

Resorts with dual affiliation. Quite a few timeshare resorts are now dual affiliated, meaning that you can join RCI, Interval

International, or both. You may want to try them both out and
see which works best for your purposes. There are pros and
cons to joining both companies.

* **Pro: Access the largest selection of resorts**. Joining
  both exchange companies lets you view and request almost
  any timeshare you could want. That doesn't mean you'll
  get it (availability and trading power are both constraints),
  but at least you can give it a try.

* **Pro: Buy vacations from both companies**. An
  economical way to vacation is via the Getaways and Extra
  Vacations offered by the major exchange companies.
  Belonging to both gives you a lot of choices. See the
  section _Extra, Getaway and Last Call Vacations_.

* **Pro: Comparison shop between the two**. You can
  search both systems to see what you can find. Sometimes
  the same resort vacation is available on both systems for
  widely different prices. Spending a little extra time on this
  can save you money.

Learn more: Save money by shopping around. I
did some sample shopping to see what I could find
at the same resort between II and RCI, and I found
that having both memberships can be worthwhile.
See the details in _Comparison shopping RCI and Interval
International_, at _TimeshareGame.com/owners-guide-links/_

* **Con: Double membership fees**. If you choose to join
  both RCI and II, you need to pay membership fees for both.
  Depending on how you use them, this may not be
  worthwhile.

* **Con: Can't deposit a timeshare with both**. Say you own
  a timeshare week at a resort that's affiliated with both
  companies, and you have memberships with both. You
  can only deposit your timeshare for exchange with one or
  the other, and once you make the deposit, your choice is
  final. You can't change your mind after that, though you
  could deposit with the other company the next year.

Here's a table showing some of the most popular timeshare companies in the US, and which of the major exchange companies they are affiliated with. You'll see that there's a split, with some big name, high quality timeshare resorts in each one.

Company	Exchange affiliation
Bluegreen Vacation Club (BVC)	Primarily RCI. Limited ability to use Interval.
Diamond Resorts International (DRI)	DRI points owners go through Interval International. Weeks may be affiliated with RCI and/or II.
Disney Vacation Club (DVC)	RCI
Hilton Grand Vacation Club (HGVC)	RCI
Marriott Vacation Club (MVC)	Interval International
RCI Points	RCI
Starwood Vacation Ownership (SVO)	Interval International
Vacation Resorts International (VRI)	RCI and/or Interval International, depending on the resort
Westgate Resorts	Interval International
Worldmark, The Club	RCI and/or Interval International

Company	Exchange affiliation
Wyndham (Club Wyndham)	Wyndham points trade in RCI. All resorts are affiliated with RCI, just a few are also affiliated with II.

Depending on which exchange company you use, you can find a lot more important information in one of these sections:

* *Option B1 - Exchanging with RCI*
* *Option B2 - Exchanging with Interval*

Using an independent exchange company

In addition to the major exchange companies, there are several independent exchange companies. These are "independent" in that they aren't tied to specific resorts. These smaller exchange companies don't have the reach or popularity of RCI or Interval International, but do have other advantages.

A few of the independent exchange companies are

* Dial an Exchange   daelive.com
* SFX Preferred Resorts   sfx-resorts.com
* Platinum Interchange   platinuminterchange.com

See the section *Organizations and Resources* for a larger list of companies.

As with most things, there are pros and cons of going with an independent vs. the major exchange companies.

Advantages of the independents

* **Avoid membership fees.** You often don't need to pay an annual membership fee like you do with RCI or II. However, even with the "free" companies there is usually a

special "Gold" membership available for an annual fee that gets you a better chance at the exchanges you want.

* **Lower fees**. The smaller exchange companies often have lower exchange fees than you would pay using RCI or II. Pay attention to details like upgrade fees, however, which can erase those savings.

* **Get around company restrictions**. Using an independent exchange company can give you the opportunity to trade for resorts that aren't part of your affiliated exchange network. Say your timeshare is only part of RCI, but you really want to stay at a resort that's only in II. One way of doing that would be to work through an independent exchange company.

* **Your deposited timeshare may last longer**. Whenever you deposit your timeshare with an exchange company, you have a certain period of time during which to use it before it expires. Working with one of the smaller exchange companies can sometimes give you a longer window of opportunity.

* **May get extra exchanges**. Sometimes the smaller exchange companies will give you additional timeshare exchanges for one deposit, as an incentive to get people to bank their timeshares. For instance, if you deposit (bank) your timeshare during a certain period of time, then you could get your regular exchange plus a credit for another week's exchange as well.

Expert tip: Watch the deals. When you're considering using one of the independent exchange companies, watch their deals before you deposit your timeshare. There are often time-limited deals that can give you extra value, so it can be advantageous to deposit in one month vs. another.

* **More bonus week selections**. Each exchange company has an inventory of bonus weeks - the extra vacation weeks you can purchase with cash rather than trading

your timeshare. Joining an independent exchange company gives you access to their selections too.

Expert tip: Joining even if you never exchange. Sometimes the bonus week selections can yield great deals on inexpensive vacations. This can make getting a free membership with one of the smaller exchange companies worthwhile, even if you never use them to trade your timeshare.

* **Request first, deposit and pay later**. Some of the smaller exchange companies allow you to put in an exchange request first, and only deposit your timeshare and pay the fee when they find a match for you. This way if you change your mind or don't find what you want, you still have control of your own timeshare. Paying the exchange fee when the trade is completed rather than up front allows you to hold onto your money longer.

Disadvantages of the independents

* **Smaller selection**. This is the most significant disadvantage. These companies don't have as many members as RCI or Interval International, so they don't have as wide a selection of timeshares available for exchanges.

* **Process can be more complicated**. Many timeshare companies have streamlined processes for dealing with RCI or Interval International, making that the easy way to go. You may need to go through more steps to use your timeshare with one of the independents, and some timeshare companies have rules which make this difficult.

* **It's not always possible**. You may not always be able to work with the company you want. For instance, SFX is known for carrying higher end timeshare properties, so they're picky about which resorts they will or won't accept for deposit.

✳ **Can't combine your weeks**. When you use RCI, you can combine deposits from multiple timeshare weeks to give you the trading power to get a more valuable exchange. The smaller timeshare companies don't have this feature, though you may be able to pay an upgrade fee to get a more desirable timeshare on your trade.

Direct exchange with another owner

This is the simplest type of timeshare exchange in concept, but not always such an easy way to go in practice. The idea is that you find an owner who has a different timeshare, and the two of you do a direct personal exchange.

Low cost. The big advantage of this approach is the low cost. You don't need to pay an exchange company any membership fee or exchange fee. You still have to pay your timeshare company for a guest certificate, so that you can assign it to your exchange partner, but that's it for the cost (unless you also pay for advertising).

May not be easy. The biggest disadvantage of this approach is the difficulty in finding a workable trade for what you want. When you do find someone offering what you would like, there's a good chance that they want something different from what you have.

Say you own a timeshare in Key West, Florida and you're looking for something in San Francisco, California. You find a timeshare owner who wants to trade their San Francisco unit, but they need to want your Key West timeshare in exchange. You may need to look for quite some time trying to find the right partner for an exchange, where both parties are happy with the destination, resort, unit size and season that the other is offering.

Places to look for a direct exchange

Close to home. Talk to your friends and coworkers. Who knows? You might be able to arrange an exchange without going very far.

TUG (Timeshare Users' Group). Among other useful features, this site has a section for members to post timeshare exchange offerings. You can browse through what's listed, or place your own ad. http://tug2.net

Timeshare Juice. This site was created to give owners a forum to facilitate and arrange direct 1-to-1 owner exchanges. You can search for the places you want to go, then make an offer on an exchange. It's up to that owner whether to accept your offer or not. timesharejuice.com

Expert tip: Use multiple avenues. If you want to do a direct owner exchange, your odds are better if you look through multiple channels. You can use all of the above sites, post your own timeshare, and keep searching through other people's offerings regularly.

Expert tip: Deteriorating trading value. The longer you keep looking for a direct exchange, the more the trading power of your timeshare can drop. For the major exchange companies, the general rule of thumb is that the sooner you deposit your timeshare, the more trading power you get for it. If you wait to deposit it, hoping for a direct owner exchange that doesn't materialize, you may find that it's not worth so much to an exchange company any more.

Expert tip: Use with a request-first search. Some exchange companies allow you to do a "request first" search, where they start a search for your exchange before you deposit your timeshare. While they are searching, you can be looking for a direct owner exchange, and see which turns up a good result first. You can't do this with a traditional "deposit first" exchange, since

your timeshare is no longer under your control once you
deposit it.

Approaches to exchange planning

There are a couple of approaches to planning your exchanges,
and your activities and timeline will be very different
depending on which you choose.

- **1 - Plan your exchange, start to finish**. In this case, you
  decide where you want to go, research the best way to
  exchange for that destination, and base all of your plans
  around this.

- **2 - Maximize your deposit, then wait and see**. With this
  approach, you know you don't want to use your own
  timeshare, but you're not sure yet where you want to go.
  You deposit it with an exchange company in time to
  maximize your trading power, then leave it open until you
  decide on a vacation.

You'll find more details on both of these, with all the necessary
activities and timing considerations, in the section *Creating
Your Timeshare Calendar*.

7. Option B1 - Exchanging with RCI

The different faces of RCI

RCI (Resort Condominiums International) is the largest timeshare exchange company in the world, and this section is devoted to the specifics of exchanging your timeshare via RCI.

Weeks and points are handled differently in RCI. There are two parts of the site, with separate logins for weeks vs. points, and different inventory. People who own multiple timeshares may end up with access to both sides, but usually you'll be working with just one side or the other. In addition, people who own with certain timeshare companies may have yet another avenue for using RCI.

When you first register for your RCI membership, you'll be set up for one of these different types of access, depending on what you own.

- **RCI Weeks**. If you own a traditional timeshare week, you log into the RCI Weeks side of the website. Continue reading in the next section, _Depositing your week with RCI_.

- **RCI Points**. If you own RCI points, you log into the RCI Points side of the website. RCI points are covered in the sections starting with _Depositing your RCI points_.

- **Portals to RCI**. Some companies like Wyndham and Hilton have their own "portals" set up to access RCI. This means that you log in via their websites rather than directly on rci.com. These situations are discussed in the section _Using RCI with other systems_.

If your timeshare is not affiliated with RCI, then you cannot join RCI or use any of these methods. Skip ahead to the section _Option B2 - Exchanging with Interval_.

Depositing your week with RCI

In order to exchange your timeshare week with RCI, the first thing you have to do is to deposit the week you own.

Depositing a fixed week. If you own a fixed week, then you have the same week every year. In this case, you can usually deposit the week yourself on the RCI website. If not, you can call your resort to make the deposit.

Depositing a floating week. If you own a floating week, you need to go through your resort to handle the deposit. It is ideal if you can request the specific week you want deposited, since that lets you choose the most "valuable" week for exchange. Some companies don't let you select your own week, and make the decision for you instead.

Your Trading Power. When you deposit your week, it will be assigned a certain "Trading Power." This is a measure that RCI uses to determine which timeshares are the most valuable, and who can trade for what. For instance, if you get 21 Trading Power Units (TPUs) for your deposit, this can be traded for other people's timeshares that are rated 21 or lower. The higher your trading power, the greater your selection of possible exchanges. This is discussed more in the section *Maximizing your RCI trading power*.

When to deposit? For RCI, the optimum time to deposit your timeshare is 9 months to 2 years before your week's start date. This gives you the maximum trading power for your timeshare. If you wait and deposit it less than 9 months in advance, you will get less trading power from the same unit, and end up with fewer exchange options. It's like losing money.

Expert tip: Depositing your week as points. If you have both an RCI Weeks membership and an RCI Points membership, then in some cases, you can use the Points for Deposit function to deposit a timeshare week into RCI Points instead of RCI Weeks. You can only do this if your week is at a resort that is not an RCI Points resort. The biggest advantages to using it as points would be (a) letting you exchange into a resort with more inventory in points than in weeks, or (b) giving you the additional RCI points you need to book a desired vacation.

Maximizing your RCI trading power

Of course you want to get the best exchanges possible for your timeshare. A key factor in doing that is knowing how to maximize your trading power.

We already talked about depositing your week at least 9 months in advance, in order to receive maximum trading power for it. There are other things you can do to maximize the value of your timeshare, too. Here are some tips.

Deposit trading power. This is the number of TPUs (Trading Power Units) that RCI assigns to the week you deposit. When you look at your deposits on the system, you'll see each week that you've deposited along with its assigned deposit trading power. For example, it may show that you have a deposit trading power of 32. This means your deposit is worth 32 TPUs, so you can exchange for any timeshare up to that number.

Factors that determine trading power. The trading power you receive for your unit determines what you can get in exchange. It's all a matter of which resorts and weeks are deemed "most valuable." Here are factors that RCI uses in calculating your trading power:

‣ Location (some destinations are in higher demand)

‣ Resort (some resorts are more luxurious)

‣ Unit type (larger units or better views are worth more)

‣ Season/week (high season and holiday weeks have higher demand)

‣ Lead time (depositing further in advance is worth more)

What you can and can't control. When you own a timeshare week, you can't do anything about the location and resort. When you made your purchase decision for that timeshare, you locked in your ownership in that resort. This is a major factor in the trading power you get, and you cannot change this. However, you may be able to control your unit type, week, and lead time, to maximize your trading power.

☑ **Change your unit type**. If you own a 2, 3 or 4-bedroom unit with a lock-off, then you can often get greater trading power in RCI by splitting it into two separate deposits. For instance, you might get 23 TPUs if you deposit your 2-bedroom timeshare as a single unit, while if you split it, you could get 17 for the studio and 19 for the 1-bedroom. That would give you a total of 36 TPUs altogether, much higher than the 23 you get for the combined 2BR unit.

Expert tip: Lock-off fees and value. Splitting a lock-off timeshare as described above can involve some extra fees. The resort may charge you a fee to lock it off, and on RCI you'll end up paying either a second exchange fee or a combination fee (more about that later). Check on the fees involved and the trading power you get for doing it one way vs. the other. If you can get 50% more trading power (not unusual), the extra fees can be well worthwhile!

☑ **Change your week**. If you own a floating timeshare, this can give you a huge advantage. Most resorts will let you request a specific week for deposit, and that's where you can work the system. For example, if you have a floating summer timeshare, the July 4 holiday week is usually worth more than other weeks. If you reserve this week and deposit it, that will pay off with more trading power.

Expert tip: Reserve first, deposit later. The way it works at many resorts is that theoretically, you can just call and say "Deposit the week starting July 2 to RCI." Sometimes you may encounter an issue, where they don't want to deposit such a prime week. In this case, it may be easier to do two separate phone calls. First, reserve the week you want, as though it's just for your own use. Then later, you can make a separate call to deposit the week you've reserved into RCI.

☑ **Change your lead time**. As mentioned before, you can maximize your trading power by depositing your week at least 9 months before the check-in date. After that, your trading power keeps dropping as you get closer to the check-in date. Here's how the calculation works:

Days in advance	% of max trade power
271+	100%
181-270	95%
91-180	90%
31-90	80%
15-30	60%
<14	45%

Expert tip: Salvaging a cancelled vacation. If you need to cancel a vacation, you can still get some value out of it with a short-notice deposit to RCI. Let's say you planned to use your own timeshare, but a family issue means you cannot go as scheduled. If you deposit your timeshare to RCI less than 2 weeks in advance, you get 45% of the max trade value, which you can use for a future vacation exchange. It's a lot less than 100%, but it's better than losing everything by letting it sit there unused.

Use the Deposit Calculator for "what if" scenarios. To make an educated decision and maximize the value of your deposit, you need to know the numbers. How much do you get if you deposit it one way vs. another? This is where you can use the Deposit Calculator on RCI. It lets you enter various start dates and unit types, and shows you the trading power you would get for each. You can experiment with different scenarios to find the precise combination that will maximize your trading power.

Expert tip: Day of the week may make a difference. Say you've run the calculator and determined that weeks 27 through 30 (July) will give you the highest amount of trading power. If your resort offers multiple check-in days for your week, test those out, too. You may find that starting your week on a Saturday gives you more trading power than starting on a Monday.

Expert tip: Work the system to double your value. It's worth spending an hour or two with the RCI calculator and a spreadsheet or pen and paper to lay out your options, run the scenarios, and document the results. It is often possible to get more than double the trading power from your timeshare by depositing the best week vs. the worst, and/or splitting your lock-off unit. A little extra effort goes a long way to maximizing the value you get from your timeshare. You'll find a place to track this on _Worksheet D - Tracking RCI Exchanges_.

Deposit trading power is locked in. Your deposit trading power is determined by when you make your deposit, relative to the check-in date of the week you deposit. Once you complete the deposit, your deposit's trading power is locked in. The date when you make your exchange, and the check-in date of the week you receive, have no impact on your assigned trading power.

Exchange trading power. This is the number of TPUs it takes to book a particular exchange. When you look through the resorts available for exchange, you will see that each one has an exchange trading power listed. For instance, if a resort shows a 2-bedroom unit with exchange trading power of 29, you would need a deposit worth at least 29 to get this exchange.

Exchange trading power varies. The exchange trading power of the weeks available on the system will vary over time. In general, as it gets closer to the check-in date, the trading power required to book one of those exchanges goes down. You might see a 1-bedroom June week at a particular resort listed for 25 TPUs, and a month later the same thing could be 22 TPUs.

Working with deposited weeks in RCI

There are some important things to be aware of when you're using RCI weeks. Your deposited timeshares are only good for so long.

Expiring deposits. When you deposit your timeshare week, you have a certain period of time to use it. With RCI, your deposit is good up to 2 years from the check-in date of the week you deposit. If you don't use it within that 2-year time, your deposit will expire. You get nothing for it if it expires, so make sure not to let that happen. Fortunately, there are ways to avoid this.
Note: Your deposit expiration date means you need to check in for your exchange by that date, not just make your exchange by that date.

Your travel window. You can use your deposit for travel any time between 12 months before your deposited week's check-in date, and 24 months after that same date. This gives you a maximum 3-year travel window, which will be shorter if you deposited your week less than 1 year in advance.

Extending a deposit. If you let a deposited week expire, you lose all the value, and you'd be paying maintenance fees for nothing. RCI gives you a limited ability to extend that deposit for a longer time, for a fee. You can extend a deposit by 1 month for $29, 3 months for $69, or 6 months for $109. You can extend the same deposit more than once, but never further than 1 year after the original expiration date. (*All fees are subject to change.*)

Deposit credits. The way trading power works, it's very common that you make an exchange that doesn't use the exact same number of TPUs that you had on your deposit. For example, if your timeshare is worth 26 trading power units, and you get an exchange that's worth 23 TPUs, that leaves you with 3 left over. These 3 "deposit credits" are the change you have left over after your transaction.

Deposit credits show up in your account just like deposited weeks do. In the above example, you would now see a deposit on your list with a trading power of 3, which you could use for a future exchange. Deposit credits have the same expiration date as the original deposit.

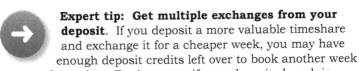

Expert tip: Get multiple exchanges from your deposit. If you deposit a more valuable timeshare and exchange it for a cheaper week, you may have enough deposit credits left over to book another week of vacation. For instance, if your deposited week is worth 31 TPUs, you could do an exchange for a timeshare worth 18. With your 13 deposit credits left over, you could do a second trade for another week.

Combining deposits. If you have multiple deposits in your RCI account, they are treated separately. For instance, you might have this year's week deposited for 21 TPUs, and another deposit with the 3 TPUs you have left over from last year's exchange. If you want to add these together, you'd get a single deposit worth 24 that you could use to exchange. This would get you more selections and higher value resorts than you could get with just 21.

Of course, there is a fee to combine your deposits, which is currently $109. But if you don't combine those leftover 3 TPUs, there's not much you can do with them, since there are few exchanges for just 3 TPUs.

Not able to travel one year. If you are unable to vacation one year, you can go ahead and bank your timeshare week with RCI. This will give you two years from that point to use it for an exchange. This deposit will still be sitting in your RCI account when you go in and bank the subsequent year. At that point, you could combine the two yearly deposits, and have double the trading power to get something extra special for your vacation.

Extend expiration dates by combining. A side benefit of combining deposits is that it automatically changes the expiration date for all of the combined TPUs to 2 years after the date you processed the combination. You could combine this year's regular deposit with 3 TPUs from last year and 5 from the year before, and this would extend all of them for a new 2-year term.

Save money by combining, not extending. If you compare combining vs. extending, you'll see that combining deposits can extend TPUs up to 2 years for $109, while extending costs $109 for just a 6-month extension. If you have more than one deposit on file, it's clearly a better deal to go for a combination.

Expert tip: Combining lets you save forever. Since combining your deposits always extends the expiration date to 2 years from the date you process the combination, this provides a way for you to make your deposits last forever. Just keep combining what you have with a new deposit the next year, and you need never face an expiration date.

Expert tip: Combining can also shrink your window. If you're working your timeshares fairly far in advance (which is advisable), then be aware that doing a combination can also shrink your expiration window in some circumstances. Here's an example:

▸ You have a July 2016 timeshare week to deposit.

▸ You make the deposit in Oct 2015, 9 months in advance.

▸ Your expiration date is July 2018 (2 years from the check-in date).

▸ At the same time in October, you combine this with some leftover TPUs.

▸ Your expiration date is now Oct 2017 (2 years from the combination date). You effectively lost 9 months from your travel window.

Work your dates. After you start using RCI, you will frequently end up with multiple deposits with different TPUs and expiration dates. Here are a few tips to help you make the most of them.

☑ If you have a floating week, always know what dates you want to reserve and deposit for the maximum trading power.

☑ Know how far in advance your resort will let you reserve that week, so you can be sure to get the most desirable dates that you want.

☑ Deposit your week to RCI 9 months or more in advance of the check-in date for maximum trading power.

☑ Combine deposits judiciously so that old deposits never expire, and new deposits don't lose too much of their travel window.

Of course, the whole purpose of depositing your week is to get an exchange. To find out how to do that, skip ahead to *Finding an available exchange with RCI*.

Depositing your RCI points

RCI Points is a separate part of the system from RCI Weeks. When you go to the website, there are two separate logins. They show two different sets of results when searching for exchanges. There are a lot of similarities, but some differences you need to know when you're using RCI Points.

Use years and record keeping. You get a certain amount of points allocated to you at the start of each "use year." These aren't calendar years, they are 12-month periods that depend on when you started your RCI points membership.

If you have a use year that runs Oct 1, 2015 through Sept 30, 2016, that is referred to as your 2015 use year since it starts in 2015, even though most of it falls in 2016.

Deposits, automatic or not. Most often, as an RCI points member, your home resort will automatically deposit your timeshare into RCI points for you at a designated date each year. There are some resorts that don't deposit your timeshare into RCI points until you specifically request it. Just make sure you know the rules for your own resort.

No maximizing trading power. With RCI weeks, if you own a floating week, you can work the system to maximize your trading power. In RCI points, you get a set number of points. There's no working the system to get an advantage.

Different types of points. It's possible to end up with multiple sets of dissimilar points, and it can get a bit confusing. For example, you might own a timeshare that's part of RCI points, and another timeshare that uses Wyndham points. While you can use both of these timeshares in RCI, they are totally separate. Wyndham points are not the same as RCI points.

Booking your home resort. If you want to stay at your home resort, then check with them on the rules. Sometimes you book it with the resort directly. At other places, even to stay there during your home week, it is still handled as a booking that goes through RCI points.

Working with RCI points

Reservation schedule. RCI has a schedule that specifies when you're allowed to book RCI points vacations.

Type of reservation	When allowed
Home week	13 months in advance
Home resort	12 months in advance
Home group	11 months in advance
Other RCI points resorts	10 months in advance
RCI weeks resorts	24 months in advance

Booking RCI points resorts vs. weeks resorts. When you do a search in your RCI points account, you will see some RCI weeks inventory that shows up in your results, too. These are resorts that are not part of the RCI points system, but since they are in RCI you are still eligible to book them. You can generally identify the weeks inventory because they will appear up to 24 months in advance, stays are always 7 nights, and check-ins are usually just one or two days a week.

Points expiration dates. Your points are allocated at the beginning of your use year. Expiration dates are counted from this date, which depends on when you started your RCI points account.

First use year. You can use any of your RCI points to exchange for any vacation you want.

Saving for year 2. Any unused RCI points from the last use year can be automatically saved for you for a second year. This means that your points really have a 2-year time limit. If you used any of your points at all, this is free. However, if you used none of your points the first year, there is a fee to save your points for year two.

Extending for year 3. If you have points you aren't using for two years, you can pay to extend them for a third year. The current fee for this is $65-$105, depending on how many points you are extending. You need to request this BEFORE your points expire at the end of that 2nd year.

After three years, they're gone. If you haven't used your points by the end of year three, they disappear. This is a hard expiration date - you cannot extend your points beyond this.

Expert tip: Weeks can last forever, points cannot. As discussed in *Working with deposited weeks in RCI*, you can use RCI's Combine Deposits feature to avoid expiration dates and extend deposited weeks forever. There is not an equivalent ability in RCI points - your points can last for only three years.

Saving vs. Extending. Saving keeps your points active for year 2, and it's automatic. Extending keeps your points active for year 3, and it's not automatic -- you need to specifically request this and pay the fee.

Combining points. Unlike RCI weeks, where you need to pay an extra fee to combine trading power from multiple deposits, your RCI points are automatically added together, giving you a total number you can use for exchanges. Points from different companies don't co-mingle - only your RCI points will be combined.

Borrowing from the future. If you want to use your points to book a vacation that requires more points than you have, you can borrow some of your points from the next use year, as long as you have paid your fees for that year.

For instance, say your timeshare gives you 45,000 RCI points per year, and that's the amount in your account. If you want to get a vacation that costs 53,000 points, you could borrow the extra 8,000 points from next year. When your next use year comes around, you would get 37,000 points (the normal 45K minus the 8K you borrowed).

Renting additional points. An alternative if you want to book a vacation that costs more points than you have, is to rent points from RCI for a cost of 2 cents per point. Rented points are temporary, and are only added to your account this one time. This is different from purchasing more points that would be yours year after year.

Continuing the same example, if you have 45,000 points and want a vacation that costs 53,000, you could rent the additional 8,000 points for $160. Then when your next use year rolled around, you would still have your full 45,000 points as always.

Limitation on renting points. There is a cap on renting points, so that you can't just buy a few points and rent tens of thousands for every vacation. The maximum you can rent is 50% of your annual points.

Transferring points between members. If you have more points than you need, you can transfer some or all of your points to another RCI Points member. Like renting points, this only applies to the one-time use of these points, vs. selling your points, which would include the recurring annual allocation.

No paying for transfers. You're not supposed to transfer points to someone else for money. If people did that, it would be the equivalent of renting additional points from another member, rather than renting them from RCI, and RCI doesn't want that. However, you may find people doing this online, even though it is against the rules.

The next thing you need to do is to find an exchange. Skip ahead to _Finding an available exchange with RCI_.

Using RCI with other systems

Some of the major timeshare companies have special ways of working with RCI. This table gives an overview of some of the differences.

Company	How to use RCI
Bluegreen Vacation Club (BVC)	To use Bluegreen points in RCI, log in through Bluegreen's RCI portal and search for a vacation. Making a reservation will debit your Bluegreen points account.
Diamond Resorts International (DRI)	Traditional weeks owners at RCI affiliated DRI resorts can deposit their week as discussed above.
Disney Vacation Club (DVC)	You can search RCI through Disney's RCI portal. Selections are limited to high quality resorts. Making a reservation will deduct the required points from your DVC account.
Hilton Grand Vacation Club (HGVC)	Log into RCI via the Hilton RCI portal, and search for a vacation. When you book something, points are deducted from your Hilton account. You can also deposit HGVC points into RCI for future use.
Marriott Vacation Club (MVC)	Not affiliated with RCI
RCI Points	See RCI points sections above.
Starwood Vacation Ownership (SVO)	Not affiliated with RCI
Vacation Resorts International (VRI)	Some VRI timeshares may be in RCI points, otherwise deposit your week to RCI weeks as discussed earlier.
Westgate Resorts	Not affiliated with RCI

Company	How to use RCI
Worldmark, The Club (WM)	Use the Worldmark RCI portal, which accesses the RCI weeks inventory. Only WM Travelshare members see the RCI points inventory. Search for a vacation, and when you make the reservation, it deducts credits from your Worldmark account.
Wyndham (Club Wyndham)	Log into the Wyndham RCI portal, which accesses RCI weeks inventory. Plus Partners owners can see RCI points inventory. Deposit Wyndham points first, or start a search first and deposit later. When you confirm a reservation, it deducts from your deposited points.

Whether you use a portal to log into RCI or go in through RCI.com directly, once you are logged in you will be using RCI to search for the vacation you want. That's the subject of the next section.

Finding an available exchange with RCI

When you want to exchange into one of the 4,000+ timeshare resorts available on RCI, you first need to find something you would like. You do this with the search features on the website. These let you search the inventory that other owners have made available to RCI, to see what you can get.

Standard search vs. On-going search

- **Standard search**. A standard search is when you search through the listings of the exchange inventory that is available right now. If you find something you want, you can book it today. The downside is that your search won't pick up timeshares that are deposited tomorrow or next month. People deposit timeshares every day, so the inventory keeps changing, but you would need to keep running manual searches to see it.

- **On-going search**. When you set up an on-going search, you specify where and when you want to go, and then the system runs the search. This on-going search keeps working for you behind the scenes, checking the timeshares that are deposited each day to see if there's something that matches your request. You don't need to log in every day, it's all automatic.

On-going searches get priority. Let's say you want to go to Cape Cod in July. You search manually every day, but the pickings are slim, since this is a popular time of year there. When somebody deposits the Cape Cod timeshare you want, RCI will first check to see if anybody has an on-going search for it. If it matches any on-going search, it will be given to them first, and will never appear on the site for your manual search to find it.

On-going searches are most likely to yield results. Sometimes you can get lucky and find a cool vacation using a standard manual search. More often, your best bet is to set up an on-going search. All you see on a standard search are the "leftovers" that make it through the gauntlet of on-going searches.

Expert tip: On-going searches in RCI points. If you are an RCI points owner, you can set up an on-going search, but it will only search the RCI weeks inventory (which you can book with your RCI points). Since weeks inventory can be booked up to 2 years in advance, you can set up one of these searches far in advance. What you cannot do with it is to search for vacations shorter than 7 days - this is for full weeks only. If you want to book shorter stays with your RCI points, you need to use the standard manual search to do that.

Deposit first vs. Request first in RCI

These are two fundamentally different ways that exchanges can happen. **Deposit first** means you deposit your timeshare into the exchange company before you request a vacation or start an on-going search. **Request first** means you submit a request and start a search, then deposit your timeshare or pay with your points after a match is found.

- **In RCI, most owners need to deposit first**. If you log into RCI.com as a traditional weeks owner, you need to deposit your timeshare with RCI before you can make an exchange or start an on-going search. With RCI points, your points are usually automatically deposited into RCI.

- **Some RCI users can request first**. As noted in _Using RCI with other systems_, owners in some timeshare companies access RCI through a portal and have different rules for their system. If you are an owner with one of these companies (such as Worldmark), you can request a search first, and then pay with your timeshare points after a match is found.

Expert tip: Request first lets you keep control of your timeshare. Let's say you own a Worldmark timeshare, but you think you'd like to travel outside that system. You can put in a request first search in RCI, and see if you get a match for a timeshare you want. If you do, then great - you can pay with your Worldmark credits then. If you don't get a match, you still have your timeshare available for a Worldmark vacation.

Expert tip: Deposit first can extend the life of your points. Say you own some Wyndham points that are going to expire soon, and you're not ready to take a vacation. You can deposit those points into RCI, and it gives you an extended period to use them for an exchange vacation.

Using the RCI search tools

Printed RCI resort directory. RCI provides a printed resort directory that gives you a catalog of vacation opportunities. The information provided is limited, and the book doesn't cover all of the RCI resorts, but it can be fun to flip through the pages, daydreaming of places you could go. The website is more comprehensive and gives you more ways to find what you want.

Standard search for exchanges. The simplest way to search RCI is to go into their Search for a Vacation area, and start looking around. There are lots of exchange possibilities out there, and the site provides different ways to narrow them down to find what you want.

Search for Exchange only. When you're looking specifically for an exchange, be sure to use the Exchange Only option. Otherwise, the system will show you other vacation opportunities that aren't exchanges. You can find more on those in the section *Extra, Getaway and Last Call vacations*.

Using the search filters. RCI provides a number of filters to help you find a timeshare vacation you want. Here are a few filters you can use:

▸ **Location**. Click on different parts of the map or on the geographical links. You can break it down by continent, country, region, state, or city.

▸ **Dates**. You can enter a date range, or just click on the month you're looking for.

▸ **Vacation type**. If you're looking for family vacations, ski trips, destinations with scuba diving, or other types of vacations, use this filter.

▸ **Resort characteristics**. These let you select resort amenities (such as a pool, or pets allowed), resort activities (such as golf or tennis), whether it's an all-inclusive resort, distance to the closest airport, star rating from user reviews, or RCI resort awards (gold crown resorts are the highest rated).

▸ **Unit characteristics**. You can select the smallest unit size you're willing to accept, the number of people it needs to sleep, or what kitchen facilities you need.

▸ **Trip characteristics**. You can select whether you want to check in on a specific day of the week, or how many nights you want to stay.

Narrow your search to fit your deposit. Viewing everything available for exchange is interesting and informative, but some of the items displayed may be out of range for you, worth more in trading power or points than what you have available. You can use the option "Show vacations that match my deposits" to narrow it down and show you just the vacations that you have enough to get. These are what you could book right now.

Expert tip: Browsing before deposit. You can browse through the listings of available exchanges, even if you haven't yet deposited your timeshare to RCI. This gives you a great idea of what's available, and what it would cost in terms of trading power or points. If you're weighing options like using your points in your own company system vs. going through RCI, or depositing your week in RCI vs. another exchange company, this can provide useful information.

Expand your search with the resort directory. When you search for exchanges, the system only displays resorts that have something available right now. There are many other RCI resorts that just don't have anything open at this time. How can you see them all? Use the online resort directory. This is the best way to find all of the resorts that fit your criteria, whether or not they have anything available right now. Unlike the printed directory, this lets you use all the search tools, and get full information on each resort.

Get the details. When your search turns up a resort that piques your interest, you can click through and find lots of information: resort details, room details, amenities, maps, area information, member star ratings and reviews, and dates available. This will also show you the trading power units (TPUs) or points required to book a specific unit and date.

Expert tip: Browsing can yield unexpected gems. Every once in awhile, spend some time just browsing through what's available. You might see something pop up that's not normally there, find a great bargain, or discover a cool vacation idea you didn't even think of, like taking a _narrowboat through the UK canals_. Finding these gems is one of the joys of timesharing.

Expert tip: Save time on your favorite searches. RCI has a useful feature that lets you save searches that you want to perform again. Say you're thinking of a vacation to Kauai next year between April and July, and you want a 1-bedroom or larger. You can set up this search and then Save to Favorite Searches. When you want to see this again, just click My Favorites and select your saved search. It's a lot faster than entering all the criteria again.

Search the discounts. There's also an option to narrow your search to discounted exchange vacations. This will show you some bargains, usually for short notice or off-season stays. You can't set up an on-going search for this.

Using the RCI resort codes. Each resort in RCI has a 4-character code that uniquely identifies it. You'll see these in your online search results and in the printed resort directory. For example, #3975 is the Coral Reef Resort in Hilton Head, SC. If you want to limit a search to specific resorts, you can enter these codes in the Advanced Search area.

See something you want? If you find something you'd like to exchange for right away, you can select it and process the exchange immediately. See the next section, _Confirming and finalizing an RCI exchange_.

Nothing you want? When a manual search on RCI doesn't show anything you want, you can either broaden your search, or set up an on-going search to find newly deposited units that meet your criteria.

Using an on-going search

Manual searches frequently don't show what you want, but don't give up. People are constantly depositing their timeshares, so there is new inventory every day. An on-going search runs for you in the background, to grab any new deposit that fits your search. This is usually the best way to get what you want.

How an on-going search works. When you start an on-going search, the system checks every day to see if new timeshares are available that match your search criteria. When something appears, you receive a notification, and can complete your exchange. Because of your on-going search, you will have first chance at this, before it ever appears for people doing manual searches.

How to set up an on-going search. You can set up a search online, or call RCI and have them set up the search for you. If you have a complicated request, calling may be the easier way to go, although it costs more to have them do it. Normally, you need to pay the exchange fee up front when you start your search.

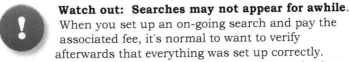

Watch out: Searches may not appear for awhile. When you set up an on-going search and pay the associated fee, it's normal to want to verify afterwards that everything was set up correctly. Unfortunately, if you immediately go back to check on your search, it may not be there. Don't panic. For some reason, searches may take a few hours before they show up in your account.

Expert tip: Plan your on-going search with the resort directory. You can set up an on-going search by location, but what if you're more selective about what you want? Perhaps you only want resorts that are right on the beach. A good way to do this is to identify the timeshares you want by using the resort directory, then enter those resort codes when you set up your search. This way your search won't match a different resort five miles from the water.

Maximizing your exchange probability. You want to set up your search so it's narrow enough that it only returns results that meet your needs. On the other hand, you're most likely to get an exchange if you keep your options fairly flexible. The broader you make your criteria, the more matches you will get.

▸ **Schedule?** If you're not tied to fixed school or work schedules, looking outside peak season is a good idea. This often gives you more availability and costs less (in TPUs or points).

▸ **Location?** It's most difficult to get a match if you're searching for one specific resort. Looking for multiple resorts, or a town or geographic area, gives you a higher probability of a match.

▸ **Unit size?** If you really need a 2-bedroom, then specify this on your search. However, if you could use anything 1-bedroom or larger, setting it up that way is more likely to get you a result.

Expert tip: Earliest searches are filled first. RCI matches on-going searches in the order they were started. If you start a search in January for summer in Hilton Head, and somebody else put in a similar request in February, yours would have priority since it was started first. The relative trading power of your deposits doesn't matter - it's just a question of who got their request in first, so start your search as soon as you can.

Start searching early for best results. Not only do earlier searches get priority, but they also have the best chance of results, just by virtue of the fact that they're running longer. Searching for 12 months gives you twice as much time to find something as searching for 6 months. Another factor is that many people try to make their deposits at least 9 months in advance, to get their full trading power. If you have your on-going search in place at that time, you could be able to snag one of those deposits.

Expert tip: Combining deposits can limit on-going searches. With RCI weeks, each of your deposits can have one on-going search running, which will match only items that require TPUs the same or less than your deposit. Let's say you have two deposits, each of which has 19 TPUs. If you keep them separate, you can run two on-going searches, and neither will match anything that costs more than 19 TPUs. If you combine them, you can get any vacation up to 38 TPUs, but you can only have one on-going search running for that combined deposit. If you have multiple deposits, combining them into one massive deposit may seem like a good idea, but it will limit your access to on-going searches.

Expert tip: Use an on-going search to get a deal. Say you really want to stay in a wonderful, high-value resort that usually requires 40 trading power, but you only have 26 TPUs on your deposit. You can set up an on-going search for this resort, tied to your 26 TPU deposit. Weeks that require 40 trading power will go by without a match, but as you get closer to the check-in date, the trading power needed for an exchange typically goes down. If somebody deposits their unit on short notice, it won't be worth as much, and you may be able to grab it with your 26 deposit. This won't always work, but sometimes it can get you a bargain.

What happens when you get a match? When a timeshare comes through that matches your on-going search, RCI will notify you by phone or e-mail. See the next section, _Confirming and finalizing an RCI exchange_.

What happens if it never matches? It's possible that an on-going search never finds a match before the time period you asked for has come and gone. If this happens, the search will automatically be cancelled, and any exchange fee you paid up front will be credited to your account. Your deposit is freed up and you can start a new on-going search if you want.

Expert tip: Change your search instead of canceling. On-going searches with an earlier start date get priority in RCI. If you have a search that is running out of time, or one you don't want anymore, you can modify it and give it new criteria that are completely different. This is basically the same as creating a new search, but modifying the old one keeps your original start date and "place in line." This gives you better odds on your revised search than if you cancel the first one and start over fresh.

Confirming and finalizing an RCI exchange

Manual search confirm or hold. When you find an exchange you want on a manual search, you can Confirm your reservation right then to finalize the deal. Sometimes you'll also get an option to put it on a 24-hour hold, however the Hold option is not available on all bookings.

On-going search auto-confirm or notify. When you create an on-going search, you can set it to Auto-confirm for you when it finds a match. If you prefer to review the results before accepting the exchange, you can set it to Notify you instead. In that case, the system will send you an e-mail when a match is found, and you have 24 hours to confirm it manually.

Complete transaction online or by phone. Unless you run into some special situation, you can complete this entire process online. It saves you money if you do, since the fees for online transactions are less than if you use the call center. If you have questions or concerns, however, it can be good to talk to a real person before you commit to the exchange.

Pay the fee(s). When you confirm your exchange, you will need to pay the exchange fee if you didn't do it already. There are also optional extras you can add, at an additional cost. There are more details in *Additional RCI opportunities*.

▸ Rent extra points to cover the transaction

▸ Purchase a Guest certificate, so someone else can use this vacation

▸ Purchase Trading power protection

Pay with your points. When you confirm the exchange, the required number of points will be deducted from your RCI points account.

Pay with your deposited week. If you're a weeks owner, you will get a deposit credit for the difference if your deposit is worth more TPUs than your exchange. This credit will show up as a new deposit in your account.

Tips for planning your RCI exchanges

Use the RCI Exchange planning tool. For RCI weeks owners, this offers you a very rough idea of what kind of trading power you'll need to book a vacation during different months of the year. You select a geographic region, and it shows the general availability and trading power requirements for that location, month by month.
Note: This is an overall average for all resorts and unit sizes in that location. Obviously the specific trading power needed for what you want could vary hugely from this number, but at least it gives you a rough idea of how hard a place will be to book.

Research point requirements. For points owners, it's easier to see what a particular resort and season will cost, since you can use the points charts on the system. The printed directory gives you points charts for many resorts, but the website is more complete, and has more up-to-date information. You can start looking at points needed well in advance of your vacation, to get an idea of how many points it will take to book what you want.

Watch the expiration dates. Both weeks and points have expiration dates you need to stay aware of. With weeks, you can use the Combine deposits feature to extend your expiration dates, as discussed in _Working with deposited weeks in RCI_. With points, you can only extend your points so long, then they expire. Whatever you do, don't let your timeshare expire unused, since that is a waste of the money and a lost opportunity.

Expert tip: On-going search to get around RCI points deadlines. With RCI points, you're only able to book RCI points resorts outside your home group up to 10 months in advance. By that time, a lot of desirable inventory in popular destinations is already gone. However, if you're able to stay for 7 nights, you can use an on-going search to check for weeks inventory up to 2 years in advance, which can give you a head start.

Additional RCI opportunities

RCI Cruises. For a different type of vacation, RCI has a wide selection of cruises available. Rather than being a straight vacation exchange, what happens is that you exchange your timeshare for a discount on the cost of the cruise.

Watch out: Shop around for cruise prices. If you're considering this option, be sure to shop around and check prices on other websites for the same or comparable cruises. Sometimes the exchange route can get you a good deal. Other times, once you factor in the cost of the timeshare you're exchanging, you'll find that you can get a better deal buying your cruise elsewhere.

Vacation homes. RCI has added vacation homes to their selections, in addition to timeshare resorts. You may see these show up in the search results, identified with a green house symbol. The selection for these is fairly limited right now, but it might expand in the future. Also, you may notice that some of the places listed as vacation homes look a lot like timeshare resorts.

Trading power protection. As discussed in _Maximizing your RCI trading power_, when you deposit a timeshare week with RCI, the value you receive in terms of trading power declines over time. The closer to the check-in date you deposit your timeshare, the less trading power you get for it.

When you cancel an exchange, you get your deposit back, however the trading power of that deposit will be recalculated based on the fact that you're now closer to (or even past) the check-in date.

Trading power protection is similar to trip cancellation insurance for your deposit's TPUs. What it does is restore your deposit to its full trading power if you do have to cancel. You will not get your exchange fee back, and it does not cover any other costs. It only affects the trading power of your deposit.

Expert tip: Pay for protection when you need it. You can buy Trading power protection when you first make your exchange, or at any time up to the day before you travel. This means that if you discover you need to cancel, you could buy the trading power protection right before you cancel. You pay a bit more this way ($89 rather than $49 when purchased up front), but you never need to pay for the protection unless you need it. _Note: I wouldn't be surprised if RCI changes this policy at some point._

Guest certificates. If you want to let someone else use a timeshare vacation that you reserved through RCI, you need to purchase a guest certificate (currently $59). The reservation will be put under their name, and they will get a confirmation from RCI. This is a great way to give somebody a very special gift!

If you're reserving multiple units for the same dates at the same resort (like you might for a family reunion), and you will be there at the initial check-in, then you should not require a guest certificate. The resort will need to see ID from the person whose name is on the reservation, so other members of your party would not be able to check in without you. If in doubt, check with the resort to confirm before paying for a guest certificate.

RCI Platinum membership. This is a higher level of membership that you can get for an additional annual fee (currently $59). You get priority access to certain resorts and sales, rebates on extra vacations and combining deposits, and perks like restaurant discounts.

> **Learn more: Is platinum a good deal for you?**
> For a full discussion and evaluation of RCI platinum membership, see
> _RCI Platinum Membership - Is it worth it?_, and
> _RCI Platinum - Still worth it in 2014?_ Find these at
> _TimeshareGame.com/owners-guide-links/_

Worksheet D - Tracking RCI Exchanges

Summary

The ability to exchange your timeshare to stay at other resorts around the world is one of the key benefits to timesharing. You can get the most value from this if you stay on top of it, depositing your timeshares at the optimal time, and setting up and monitoring your on-going searches.

This worksheet is for tracking deposits and exchanges that go through RCI weeks. If you have RCI points, use _Worksheet C - Tracking Points_. Exchanges through Interval International or one of the other companies are tracked on a different sheet (_Worksheet E - Tracking II exchanges_).

How to use this worksheet

- **Sections by timeshare year** - Down the left side, you have groups of rows separated into years. The years are based on the check-in date of the week you deposit. If you have a 2016 timeshare week, it goes under 2016, even though you might deposit it with RCI in 2015, and use it for a vacation in 2017. Keeping every deposit in its original year helps to keep this all straight.

- **Weeks deposited** - Whenever you deposit a week into RCI, enter the deposit here, along with details like the date of your transaction, the unit type and check-in date, the Rel# (a tracking number used by RCI), the number of TPUs you got for that deposit, and the expiration date for those TPUs.

- **On-going searches** - When you set up an on-going search enter the details of it here. A search needs to be tied to a specific deposit, so enter it right below the associated deposit. You can also color code them together so that it's easy to see which deposits are tied up with which searches.

- **Search modifications** - If you modify your search later on, enter another row for the modified search. This is helpful so you can see the history of what happened.

- **Vacations reserved and completed** - When you get an exchange, enter the details about it here, including the destination, transaction date, check-in date, and unit size. Also enter the TPUs which were spent on this exchange, and subtract that from what you had, to see the balance left over.
  Note: If you had an ongoing search, mark the search as matched and close it out once you have the vacation booked.

- **Deposit credits** - If you end up with TPUs left over from an exchange, this is a deposit credit. It gets its own line on the spreadsheet because it has its own Rel# in RCI and it is treated like a new deposit. If your deposit credit has enough TPUs, you could book another exchange with it. If

it's too small for that, you can combine it later with
something else.

- **Combining deposits** - If you combine two or more
deposits, then enter the combination here. You will end up
with one new deposit, with its own Rel#, TPUs, and
expiration date, which can now be used for searches and
exchanges. Mark the old deposits you combined as closed.

- **Open deposits** - You can have multiple open deposits at
one time. It's good to highlight these in yellow, since these
are what you have to work with right now. Be sure to
watch the expiration dates, and find a way to use these
before then, so they don't go to waste.

- **Fees paid** - Whenever you pay an RCI fee for an exchange
or combination, enter the amount and date on the line for
the associated transaction. You may pay a fee when you
initiate an ongoing search, so when the exchange comes
through you know it's already been paid.

- **Dates to watch** - If you have certain dates you need to pay
attention to, note them on the spreadsheet and highlight
them. Examples could include:

    ▸ Deposits that have an expiration date coming up

    ▸ Dates you want to deposit a week to maximize your
      trading power.

    ▸ Ongoing searches that are approaching your desired
      trip date (so you can make alternate plans if you don't
      find a match)

Usage tips

- **Review regularly** - Check this regularly, and keep it up to
date. This helps you get the best exchanges, by staying on
top of what you have available for exchange, what searches
you have running, and what your critical dates are.

- **On and off usage** - You may have a timeshare that you
exchange with RCI one year, but another year you use it
yourself or exchange it with a different method. You may

want to make a note here of how you used it in the non-RCI years, just so you remember what happened.

- **Multiple timeshare weeks** - If you have multiple timeshare weeks in RCI, track them all together on this spreadsheet. II exchanges are tracked on a different worksheet.

Links to worksheets

- SAMPLE worksheet - This copy is filled out with sample data for different types of timeshares. The data is not real - it's purely for illustration purposes, so you can see how the spreadsheet works.

- BLANK worksheet - For your own use.

- Worksheets are at
  TimeshareGame.com/owners-guide-links/

8. Option B2 - Exchanging with Interval

Deposit first vs. Request first in II

Interval International (II) lets you choose which method you want to use for your timeshare exchange - Deposit first, or Request first. Here's how they work.

- **Deposit first**. You deposit your timeshare into Interval, giving them full rights to it. They can now make it available to someone else for exchange. Your deposit has a certain trading power assigned to it, which you can use to make an exchange in II. **Note:** In II you never see your trading power, it is only used behind the scenes.

- **Request first**. You start searching for a vacation on Interval before you deposit your timeshare with them. Once you find an exchange that you want, you deposit your timeshare at that time to finalize the exchange.

There are pros and cons to both methods. This table shows some of the key differences between these two exchange methods, and can help you decide when to use one or the other.

	Deposit first	Request first
Rights to your timeshare	You lose all rights to your timeshare once it's deposited. You can no longer use it yourself, exchange it via a different company, give it away, or rent it out.	You retain control of your timeshare. If you don't find what you want, you're free to use it yourself, exchange it through a different company, give it away, or rent it out.

	Deposit first	Request first
Your trading power	Your trading power is locked in when you make the deposit, and doesn't shrink as its check-in date approaches and passes.	Your week's trading power shrinks as its check-in date approaches. When that date passes, it loses all value.
How early can you start?	Place deposit up to 2 years before your week's check-in date.	Place request up to 2 years before your week's check-in date.
How long can you use it?	Your can make exchanges from 2 years before to 2 years after your week's check-in date.	You can make an exchange and deposit your week up to 14 days before your week's check-in.
Travel window	4-year travel window: 2 years before your week's check-in to 2 years after.	2-year travel window: 2 years before your week's check-in date, up to that date.

Expert tip: Running multiple simultaneous searches. You can have a request-first vacation search running with multiple exchange companies at once. As soon as one of them turns up an exchange you want, just deposit your week with that company and cancel the other searches.

Depositing your week with Interval

Depending on what and where you own, there are different ways this can work. Here are the points to consider.

If you own a fixed week, you may be able to deposit your week directly on the Interval International website. Once your timeshare is registered with your II account, it will show up on your account under My Units. You can click on Deposit Unit from there to make the deposit. You can also call to make the deposit by phone.

If you own a floating week, you usually need to make a reservation at your resort first, then get it deposited into Interval. This gives you some flexibility to maximize your trading power. The resort may handle the deposit for you, or they may give you a reservation number so that you can make the deposit yourself with II.

Floating weeks don't always give you a choice. In some floating week timeshares, you cannot select a specific week to reserve and deposit. Instead, when you tell your resort you want to deposit your timeshare into II, they select a week and deposit it for you.

No deposits within 14 days. You cannot deposit your week into Interval less than 14 days before its check-in date. No deposits are accepted that late. If you get to that stage, you need to use the week yourself or make alternate plans.

Expert tip: Last minute deposits can use RCI, not II. If you're within two weeks of check-in and have missed your chance to deposit your week to Interval, you may still be able to deposit it with RCI if your timeshare is affiliated with both companies. In RCI, you can deposit a week less than 14 days before check-in and get 45% of the maximum trading power. That's not ideal, but you can't get anything at all with II.

Some of the major timeshare companies have special ways of working with Interval International. This table gives an overview.

Company	How to use Interval International
Bluegreen Vacation Club (BVC)	Bluegreen points are RCI only, but weeks may be able to be deposited in Interval as described above.
Diamond Resorts International (DRI)	Traditional weeks owners at II-affiliated resorts can deposit their weeks as above. Owners with club points request first, then pay for exchanges with DRI points.
Disney Vacation Club (DVC)	Not affiliated with Interval
Hilton Grand Vacation Club (HGVC)	Not affiliated with Interval
Marriott Vacation Club (MVC)	Weeks owners can reserve their week and deposit it into II as above. Points owners request first, then pay for the exchange with their Marriott points.
RCI Points	Not affiliated with Interval
Starwood Vacation Ownership (SVO)	Deposit weeks in II as above, except that Starwood deposits a generic week (average of the season you own). Staroption points are not used in II.
Vacation Resorts International (VRI)	Owners at II-affiliated resorts can deposit their week as described above.
Westgate Resorts	Owners can deposit their week as described above.
Worldmark, The Club (WM)	Use deposit first or request first in II. When the deposit is made, you give up Worldmark points, and Worldmark gives II a week worth that many points.

Company	How to use Interval International
Wyndham (Club Wyndham)	A few Wyndham resorts allow weeks to be deposited in Interval. Wyndham points are not used in II.

Maximizing your II trading power

Trading power in Interval International. Every timeshare that goes to Interval for an exchange is assigned a certain trading power, based on the destination's supply and demand, resort quality and amenities, demand for the season and week, unit size, and more. The company's goal is to give you an exchange of comparable value to the timeshare you're trading.

It's all behind the scenes. Trading power on Interval is all behind the scenes, hidden from view. Unlike RCI, you never see a number showing you the trading power of your unit, or the required trading power for what you hope to get. You can generally assume that a larger unit is worth more than a small one and high season is worth more than low, but the actual calculations are secret. You can only interpret this from the selections you see. See more in _Finding an available exchange with II_.

Interval's Travel Demand Index (TDI). Every resort in II has an associated Travel Demand Index chart. This chart shows the relative demand for that location, week by week through the year. The higher the TDI, the higher the demand has historically been for that week.

Deposit the highest TDI week you can. If you deposit a high-TDI week, you have greater trading power than if you deposit a lower TDI week. If you have a floating timeshare week, try to reserve the week with the highest possible TDI within the season that you own. Whether you own high season or low season, there is usually room within that season to select a week that maximizes your trading power.

Expert tip: Whenever you can, choose your own week. In some systems, you have the option of selecting a week yourself to deposit, or allowing the timeshare company to deposit a week for you. If you have a choice, always pick the week yourself, so you can maximize your own trading power. The company has no incentive to select a good week for you, and you could end up with a less valuable deposit.

Expert tip: Special occasions can supersede TDI. The Travel Demand Index is based on historical demand. Sometimes, special occasions can override these past averages. For example, holidays like Easter fall on different weeks in different years. Big events like the Superbowl can turn an off-season week into the biggest week of the year. It pays to consider special occasions when selecting the highest value week to reserve.

Note: If you're lucky enough to book something like Superbowl week, then you might consider renting it out for cash rather than depositing it. You'll find more about that in *Renting out your timeshare*.

Deposit early for maximum trading power. If you deposit your week with Interval a year before its check-in date, you will get the maximum trading power for it. If you wait and deposit closer to the check-in date, the trading power goes down as that date approaches.

Expert tip: Use deposit first to lock in your trading power. While using a request-first search does have advantages, the downside is that your trading power can drop off as months go by while your search is running. When you deposit first, your trading power is locked in at the time you deposit.

Watch out: Limitations on deposits less than 2 months out. If you deposit your week less than 60 days before its check-in date, that week is designated as a Flexchange deposit, and has serious restrictions on its use. Find out more about this in the section *Using Flexchange*. If at all possible, be sure to deposit further in advance than this.

Splitting your lock-off or not. When you have a lock-off timeshare, you have options. Splitting the lock-off gives you two deposits, which will get you two exchanges, but each of them will be lesser value exchanges. Keeping it together gives you just one deposit and one exchange, but it has more trading power to pull a bigger, better exchange.

Bonus weeks (Accommodation Certificates). Interval will sometimes notify you, online or by snail mail, that you can get a bonus week if you deposit your timeshare by a designated date. This is usually an incentive to deposit your week early rather than waiting. If you deposit when such an offer is in place, you can get an extra week's exchange out of the deal. These are limited in scope, but can be a nice bonus. Find out more about bonus weeks in *Getting extra weeks with II*.

Expert tip: Use deposit first to get a bonus week. If you see a bonus week offer from Interval, you need to go ahead and deposit your week if you want to take advantage of it. Going for a request-first search instead can mean losing this opportunity. You may have other important reasons for making that decision, but be aware of the pros and cons.

Expert tip: Studio deposits will rarely receive a bonus week. Larger units receive offers of bonus weeks more often than smaller units, and studios are not often eligible for a bonus offer. You may find that depositing a full lock-off together qualifies for a bonus week, while splitting it does not.

Working with deposited weeks in II

There are some important things to be aware of when you deposit a timeshare with Interval.

Expiring deposits. If you use the request-first method, your deposit is "used up" as soon as you use it to complete the exchange. On the other hand, when you deposit your timeshare first, it has an expiration date which is 2 years from the check-in date of the week you deposit. If you don't complete your exchange and travel by that date, your deposit will expire and lose all value.

Extending a deposit. What if you let your expiration date go by? You can pay a fee to extend it, but there are some serious considerations.

▸ You can extend your deposit for 3, 6 or 12 months. The current fees for that are $69, $99, and $189. (All fees are subject to change.)

▸ You must process an extension within 3 months of the expiration date, or you lose your chance to extend.

▸ Extended deposits are treated like Flexchange deposits, which is a major limitation. See more about that in _Using Flexchange_.

▸ You can extend a second time, but only if you extend within 3 months of the previously extended expiration date.

No combining deposits. Unlike RCI, you cannot combine multiple smaller deposits to give you a single deposit with more trading power. In RCI, you could take 5 separate studio deposits, and combine them into a super trader. In II, you can't combine them - they would stay as 5 small deposits.

Not able to travel one year. If you are unable to vacation one year, you can go ahead and deposit your timeshare week with Interval. This gives you a travel window up to two years from the check-in date of your week.

Work your dates. You may end up with multiple deposits in II, with different units and/or dates. Track your dates carefully in order to get the most value from your timeshare.

☑ If you have a floating week, know what week to reserve for the maximum trading power, and how far in advance you can make that reservation.

☑ If you want to lock in maximum trading power, use the deposit-first approach, and deposit your week as far in advance as you can.

☑ If you're keeping your options open, you can use the request-first system. Give yourself a cut-off date to re-evaluate and make other plans if you haven't found a match. If you keep it running too long, your trading power can disappear.

☑ Make sure to deposit more than 60 days in advance if at all possible, to avoid flex deposit restrictions.

☑ Track expiration dates to make sure you don't lose a deposit.

Finding an available exchange with II

Instant exchange vs. Exchange request. There are two ways you can go about finding an exchange you want in Interval. The simplest is to search online and see what's out there. This is an instant exchange, because you can find something and instantly confirm it.

The other way of doing it is to create a pending exchange request in the system. Use this method if what you want isn't available right away. Timeshares are deposited every day, and what you want could come into the system next week or 3 months from now. Once you have an exchange request in place, it keeps searching behind the scenes for you, looking for something that fits your criteria.

Finding an instant exchange

Searching for an instant exchange. You can use the online search tools in the Exchange tab on Interval's website to browse through the inventory of available II exchanges. There are a few parameters you need to enter.

▸ **Select your timeshare**. You need to pick what you want to exchange, under "My Units." This shows you timeshares you have already deposited, as well as those that the system thinks are available for deposit. (It won't know if you've already deposited this with a different exchange company.)

▸ **Select the destination**. Unless you have specific resorts in mind, it's usually easiest to do this with the "Use Map" option.

▸ **Select the date range**. You can search dates from tomorrow up to two years in the future.

▸ **Set how many people are traveling**. This will control the unit sizes that you see in the results.

What you see depends on your trading power. The results are filtered to show you only those that fit the trading power of your deposit. Any exchanges that would require more trading power than you have simply don't appear. The upside is that you can immediately book anything that shows up. The downside is that when you don't see a result, you don't know whether it isn't available at all, or you just don't have enough trading power to get it.

Learn more: How filtering works in Interval vs. RCI. Find out more about how II filters your search results in various ways, and what it may be leaving out of your results. See *RCI vs. Interval - Filtering and transparency*, at *TimeshareGame.com/owners-guide-links/*

Expert tip: Search with more than one unit. You can get an idea of relative trading power by doing the same search with more than one unit, if you have that possibility in your II account. For instance, if you have a 3-bedroom lock-off that splits into a 1-bedroom and a 2-bedroom, you can try the same search with the 1BR, 2BR, and 3BR and see what different results you get. This can be quite enlightening.

Expert tip: Search with a fake deposit. What if you don't have a deposit with II to exchange yet? Select an undeposited unit that appears on your list, and click Vacation exchange for it. Enter a phony reservation number like 123456. You can continue with the search as though this had already been deposited. This is useful if you want to see what you could get before committing your timeshare to an II deposit. Of course, you can't confirm any exchange yet if you're searching with a fake deposit.

Using an exchange request

Setting up a pending exchange request. Don't worry too much if you don't see what you want with an online search. Pending exchange requests get priority, so many desirable units are snatched up for pending requests and you won't see them in the online search results. To set up an exchange request, just select a unit to use, and click on Place a Request, then follow the prompts. It's pretty straight forward, though there are a few things to note.

▸ **Deposit first or request first**. You can set up a pending request either way. See _Deposit first vs. Request first in II_ for considerations when you're making this decision.

▸ **Time frame**. The farthest out you can search is 2 years from the date you set up the request, or 2 years from the date of the week you're exchanging, whichever comes first. For request-first, you cannot search beyond the check-in date of your timeshare week.

▸ **At least 3 possibilities**. You can't create a search unless you give it at least 3 options to search for. This can be 3 different resorts for one time period, one resort with 3 time periods, or 2 resorts for 2 time periods.

▸ **You can make it complicated**. The 3 options rule is a minimum. You are free to provide a long list of resorts on your request, or a complex assortment of resorts and time periods.

▸ **Thursdays**. No matter what date you select for the start of your search, II will change it to the Thursday before the date you entered. This means it will match check-in dates on Friday, Saturday, or any other day that week.

Watch out: II search dates are confusing. Whatever dates you enter on your search, Interval will change them to the nearest Thursdays. You may enter a request starting Saturday March 15, then go back to look at your search and find it says Thursday March 13. For the check-in date, this means you could be confirmed into a week starting any day, but typically you'll get a Friday, Saturday, or Sunday check-in.

The check-out dates are even more confusing. First, the date you enter will be moved forward or back to the nearest Thursday. Then, even though you have it listed as a final check-out date on your request, you may be confirmed for a week that extends beyond this date - typically to the following Friday, Saturday or Sunday.

Here's an example:
▸ Enter a pending request with dates March 14-24 (Friday to Monday), because that is the date range you have available for travel.

▸ Interval changes this to move both start and end dates to the nearest Thursdays, making it March 13-27.

▸ They then confirm a week with dates March 22-29. Even though the request had a a check-out date of March 24, the system can match this to a week that extends 5 days beyond that.

Expert tip: Plan II exchange requests with Thursdays. You can avoid some unwanted surprises by setting up your request start and end dates on Thursdays. This way II won't change the dates once you enter them. Just remember that you could be checked in or out on the Friday, Saturday or Sunday following the start and end dates you enter. If in doubt, you can always call an II rep to set up your request, but you save $20 on the exchange fee when you do it yourself online.

Expert tip: What if you want a specific check-in day? Say you only want a Saturday check-in, but II changed your search to start on Thursday. You can call II to have them make a note of your Saturday preference on your search. The only way to be perfectly sure, however, is to monitor your account and decline any non-Saturday check-in that they give you.

Priority on filling exchange requests. When a new timeshare week is deposited in Interval, and there are multiple pending exchange requests that it could match, Interval goes through these steps to decide who gets it.

1. There is a company preference that sometimes comes into play, so that owners of a company get priority for exchanges in their own company. See more about this in *Company preference in II*.

2. Whoever's exchange request has a deposit with the greatest trading power gets priority. If somebody else's timeshare deposit has more trading power than yours, they get priority, even if you started your request sooner.

3. For multiple requests with equivalent trading power, the request placed first gets priority.

Maximizing your chances with II exchanges

Increase odds with an earlier request. Earlier requests give you time to find a match, before other people get competing requests in place. Searching for 15 months is more likely to get results than searching for 9 months or 3 months. Also, since earlier requests can get priority over later ones (if they have equivalent trading power), this is the simplest way to boost your chances of getting the exchange you want.

Expert tip: Starting your request more than a year out. Starting a search more than 1 year in advance puts you in a good position. A year in advance is a fairly common time for people to deposit timeshares, when they want to maximize their own trading power. If you already have a pending exchange request in the system, you'll have the best chance of nabbing those deposits when they come in.

Expert tip: Pending requests and bulk deposits. Some timeshares do bulk deposits, where they deposit many units and dates for the same timeshare at once. Having an exchange request in place gives you an excellent chance of grabbing one of these timeshares when the bulk deposit goes through.

Increase odds with a broader request. Flexibility is the key here. If you're looking for a particular resort in the Cayman Islands for a certain week next year, your chances are not nearly as high as if you open up that search to all resorts in the country, or expand it to a 2-month timeframe.

Expert tip: What if you only want a single resort? On an exchange request, Interval makes you enter at least 3 options (combinations of resort and time frame). What if there's really only one resort and week that fits your needs? A trick is to put impossible requests in the other two slots to meet their requirements. Try something like the Westin St. John for Christmas week, or the Manhattan Club Penthouse Suites over New Year's Eve. Your chances of getting one of these are up there with winning the lottery. Since those two will never match, the only thing you could get out of this request will be the single item you want. Of course, a broader search is far more likely to get you a match, but if you really only want one place, this is a way to do it.

High TDI weeks will be hardest to get. Each destination has a Travel Demand Index chart. Weeks with a high TDI typically have more people searching for them (i.e. greater competition), and the trading power required to get them on exchange is greater. You'll find it easier to get weeks with a lower TDI (either shoulder season or low season), especially if your deposit does not have a very high trading power. Of course, you can always request the peak weeks, and take other steps to try to maximize your chances.

Better odds with smaller units. Let's say you deposit a 1-bedroom timeshare with II. You prefer to stay in a 1-bedroom unit when you travel, but if you're willing to stay in a studio, putting in a request for a studio will give you better odds of finding a match. You need to decide what's more important - getting the destination or resort you want, or getting the larger unit? Consider your options and set up your request accordingly.

No unit size upgrades on an exchange request. You cannot submit an exchange request for a larger unit than the week you're using for your deposit. Typically this means that if you're exchanging a studio, you can only search for studios. If you deposit a 1-bedroom, you could search for studios or 1-bedrooms, but not 2-bedrooms or larger.

Expert tip: Instant exchanges can give upsize trades. For instant exchanges there are no unit size restrictions, it's just based on trading power. It's quite possible for a high-season 1-bedroom timeshare (or even a studio), to have more trading power than a 2-bedroom in low season or at a lesser resort. This means you can often trade up in size, though you may need to trade down in season or resort quality to make up for it. You can do this via an instant exchange, but not on a pending request.

Expert tip: Resorts with only 2-bedroom units. This is a backdoor that can sometimes get you around the unit size restriction on pending exchange requests. There are some resorts that only have 2-bedroom units. You can select such a resort on your pending request, even if your deposit is only a studio or

1-bedroom. As long as you have enough trading power for the exchange, this approach may get you a unit size increase.

Watch out: Getting a match you don't want. It is possible to get a pending exchange request filled and finalized without your knowledge (see *Confirming and finalizing an II exchange*), so it pays to be careful with what you enter on the request. For instance, if you have everything in Myrtle Beach on your request, you may find that it gives you a resort you don't really want. You can prevent this by doing more research up front, and omitting any resorts you don't want. Obviously, the more you limit your selections, the more you limit your chances of a match, so there is a trade-off to consider.

Keep searching yourself. Even when you have an exchange request in place, it never hurts to search manually now and then. There are numerous anecdotal accounts where people found what they wanted online before it matched their pending exchange request. This isn't supposed to happen - pending requests are supposed to be filled first. Nevertheless, it appears that sometimes something slips through, so it never hurts to check.

Expert tip: Save favorite resort codes in a text file. When you perform the same search over and over, it can save a lot of time to keep the resort codes you want in a text file. Just type the 3-character resort codes for the places you want, separated by commas. For instance, if you're looking for Marco Island, you might have "*EGL, MMI, SCM*" as your list. Then when you do a search, just copy and paste the codes from your text document into the search criteria. It's much faster!

Expert tip: Retrade if you find something better. Once you book an exchange, you may still want to keep searching occasionally to see if you could get something better. Sometimes a better option can pop up near your check-in date as a last-minute exchange. For instance, you might have accepted a studio, then find a 1-

bedroom later on. If you find something you like better than what you have booked, you can do a Retrade to get it. Unless you've purchased ePlus (more on that in _Other opportunities with II_), you will have to pay another exchange fee for the retrade, but sometimes it may be worth it.

Using Flexchange

Flexchange means short notice. Flexchange is a term unique to Interval International. It designates exchanges or deposits that are made less than 60 days before the check-in date.

It's not always obvious. Flexchange can be a bit confusing to people new to II. While you may see sometime like "Featured Flexchange destinations" on the II home page, there are less obvious ways to view that inventory, too. If you just use the normal exchange search with a date range up to 59 days from today, you are seeing Flexchange choices, even though you don't see that term on the screen. If you do a search that encompasses the next 6 months, everything that shows up with a check-in date less than 60 days from your search is Flexchange, even though it won't be identified as such.

Flexchange exchanges. Any exchange you make for a timeshare less than 60 days before your travel date is a Flexchange exchange. You can request such an exchange any time from 24 hours to 59 days before the check-in date of the timeshare stay you're booking.

You can use any deposit for a Flexchange exchange. It doesn't matter whether you deposited your timeshare 18 months or 3 weeks before your check-in date. Any deposit is usable for a Flexchange exchange.

Expert tip: Using Flexchange for up-trades. The trading power of any week deposited goes down as it nears the check-in date. That means that a week deposited during the Flexchange period, or a week that becomes available due to a late cancellation, doesn't have very high trading power. You can get some amazing trades during Flexchange if you search now and then. Timeshares can pop up that you wouldn't normally have enough trading power to see. Using your 1-bedroom to book a luxury 2-bedroom in Hawaii? Stranger things have happened in Flexchange.

Flexchange for bargain vacations. Bargain hunters love searching through the Flexchange opportunities. It's like a constantly changing treasure trove of opportunities. The keys to making this work are (a) you need to be able to travel on short notice, (b) you need to be able to book something quickly when you find it, and (c) you need to consider the cost of travel in your calculations. Destinations that require air travel may end up offsetting a bargain exchange with high last-minute airfare.

Expert tip: You've got to move fast. If you're browsing through the Flexchange opportunities and see a great deal, you need to move fast. If you wait to check with your spouse, there's a good chance that the exchange you want will be gone by the time you get back to it. Good deals can disappear very quickly.

Flex deposits. If you deposit your timeshare week less than 60 days before your check-in date, that deposit is categorized as a Flex deposit. Since you cannot deposit less than 14 days in advance, this means the Flex deposit window is 59 to 14 days before the start of your week.

Flex deposits can only get Flex exchanges. If you make a Flex (short notice) deposit, then you can only get a Flexchange (short notice) exchange with it. You cannot book anything more than 59 days in advance.

No pending exchange requests with Flex deposits. Another limitation of Flex deposits is that you cannot set up a pending exchange request attached to one. You need to rely solely on manual searches and instant exchanges.

Watch out: Avoid Flex deposits. The limitations on a Flex deposit are significant, and it's wise to avoid ending up in this situation if you have any choice. The difference between getting your deposit in 60 days in advance and 59 days in advance means that it's worth tracking your dates to make sure you end up with a fully usable timeshare deposit.

Company preference in II

Some companies give preference to their owners. Interval International allows some companies to give a preference to people who exchange another week from the same company.

Marriott gives a 21 day preference period. When a Marriott week is deposited, for 21 days it is only available to people who are exchanging another Marriott. Only if this 21 day period passes without someone picking up the exchange, will this open up for other exchangers.

As a Marriott owner, this preference works in your favor when you want to stay at another Marriott. Obviously, if you own in a different system, the preference period makes it much more difficult for you to exchange into high-demand Marriott timeshares.

After the preference period, pending exchange requests are next in line. If a deposited week makes it through the Marriott preference period without being snatched up, it will move on to the pending exchange requests from non-Marriott owners. If there are no pending requests that match and have enough trading power for the exchange, then and only then, will this timeshare appear in the online search results for non-Marriott exchangers.

Starwood gives the same kind of preference period. When a Starwood week is deposited, it goes into a preference period of about 20 days for other Starwood exchangers, before it's made available to other II members. This works just the same as the Marriott preference period.

Expert tip: Cancellations can skip the preference period. Every so often, a high-demand Marriott or Starwood week will show up in general availability, rather than being picked up during the preference period. One explanation for this is that it was a cancellation, where the preference period runs from the date of the original deposit. For example, a prime Starwood week could be deposited in March, and picked up for an exchange the next day, during the preference period. If that exchange was cancelled in August, the unit would be past the preference time, and could show up for other people.

Confirming and finalizing an II exchange

Confirming an instant exchange. When you're searching for an instant exchange and see something you want, just click the Exchange button. You will need to pay the exchange fee, and accept or decline any optional extras like ePlus (more on that later). When the transaction is complete, you will receive an e-mail confirmation of your reservation.

Once an instant exchange is complete, it's a done deal. When you do an instant exchange, it's done. You don't have any cancellation period to change your mind without a penalty. If you decide you want something different, you can do a retrade later.

Expert tip: Use your lowest possible deposit. If you have multiple units you can select for an exchange, try them out and use the lowest value unit that will let you make this exchange. For example, if you see an instant exchange with a 2-bedroom deposit, can you also see the same exchange with a 1-bedroom? If so, using your 1-bedroom would let you save the larger unit for a different exchange.

Expert tip: Use deposits near expiration first. If you have multiple units with different expiration dates, and one of them is nearing its end, then using that one for your instant exchange can be a wise plan, even if it is a larger or better unit. It's a waste to let anything expire.

Matching a pending exchange request. When Interval finds a match for a pending request you have in the system, they will automatically confirm it, and send you an e-mail confirmation. You have 24 hours in which to cancel this without penalty. After that 24 hours, the exchange is complete.

Watch out: Monitor your pending requests. It's easy to miss a confirmation if you are traveling and not monitoring your e-mail every day. If this happens, you can miss your 24-hour cancellation period, and end up with an exchange that's not really what you want. When you have a pending request in the system, it's wise to check e-mail or check the Interval website each day, so you're aware when you get a match.

Watch out: Interval sometimes calls with non-matches. II occasionally calls you when your exchange request does not have a match (though not when you do have a match). They will sometimes suggest something else that's kind of like what you requested, rather than exactly what you asked for. If you entered a selection of resorts right on the coast, you could get a call wanting to give you something 20 miles inland. Be careful to check out exactly what they are suggesting before you proceed.

Getting extra weeks with II

Bonus weeks (Accommodation certificates). As mentioned in *Maximizing your II trading power*, sometimes Interval offers a bonus week for depositing your timeshare by a certain deadline. This isn't the only time you'll get a bonus week, which is also referred to as an Accommodation Certificate, or AC for short. Sometimes you can get a bonus week in a special promotion, or even get one out of the blue, just for being a good customer. Here's an overview of how they work.

▸ You get an extra week for the AC deposited in your II account, which you can use to book another exchange.

▸ To book the AC bonus week, you need to pay a fee, but you don't need to give up your own timeshare.

▸ There are limitations on what exchanges this is good for. There's a booking deadline which is usually restricted to fairly short notice, and a grid of locations where you can use the week.

▸ The fee varies with different AC offers. Sometimes you pay just an exchange fee, while other times the fee depends on the unit size you're booking.

Some people find the Interval bonus weeks more useful than others, but when it works for you, it is an inexpensive vacation that doesn't require exchanging your own timeshare.

Learn more: Ins and outs of using bonus weeks. Find out more details about how you can get an AC bonus week, how the limitations on them work, and some tips on how to make the most of them, at _How to Get Bonus Timeshare Weeks on II_, at _TimeshareGame.com/owners-guide-links/_

XYZ (2-for-1) exchanges. This is a hidden program that Interval offers that can give you an extra week of vacation whenever you make an exchange. This isn't documented on their website or in their handbook. You just need to know to call in and ask for it, and you can start getting almost-free vacation weeks! Here's how you can get these 2-for-1 exchanges.

▶ The only cost to book an XYZ is that you need to pay another exchange fee. You don't actually need to exchange anything for it, so it's a nearly-free vacation week.

▶ Each XYZ exchange is associated with one normal exchange.

▶ You must have your normal exchange confirmed and paid before you're eligible for the associated XYZ.

▶ Like bonus weeks, there are some strict limitations on booking an XYZ. You are usually restricted to off-season travel and/or locations with an abundant supply of timeshares.

▶ You can only get an XYZ for the unit size of your original exchange, or smaller.

▶ There is a grid that shows which destinations are available in which months for an XYZ. This grid goes just a few months into the future.

▶ Unlike bonus weeks, the XYZ grid is not publicly available, so there's no way to know what you can get without calling Interval.

▶ You must **book the XYZ before** you travel on the original exchange, and **travel on the XYZ after** you travel on the original exchange.

Like bonus weeks, 2-for-1 XYZ exchanges don't work well for everyone due to the significant restrictions on them, but when they do, it can be a wonderful thing, giving you an extra vacation week for a minimal cost.

Watch out: Inconsistent employee knowledge. A complication with XYZ's is that the people at Interval are not consistently trained on them. You may call in and get somebody who doesn't know anything about XYZ's. Your second call could find somebody who explains the rules one way, and your third call could get somebody who explains it differently.

Expert tip: Note the name and extension of an XYZ expert. Once you find somebody knowledgeable at Interval who helps you book an XYZ, make a note of that person's name and extension number. This way, the next time you want to book an XYZ you can get straight to an expert, rather than wasting time talking to others who don't know the system.

Expert tip: Work the XYZ date range. To get an XYZ 2-for-1 exchange, you need to (1) Confirm a normal exchange, (2) Book the XYZ over the phone **before** your check-in date for the original exchange. (3) Travel on the XYZ exchange **after** you travel on the original exchange.

Since the grid only goes a few months into the future, this gives you an effective window of about 3 months or so after your original exchange to take the XYZ (depending on when the grid is made available). To make best use of an XYZ, you can start planning this in advance, knowing the travel window you can use, and when you'll need to book a reservation.

Here's an example:

▸ Say you booked a regular II exchange week in Colorado, August 8-15.

▸ For an XYZ, you'd need to **book it before** Aug 8, and **travel after** Aug 15.

▸ You'd like to visit Scottsdale in September, which is not high season.

▸ The XYZ grid for September could come out around May. Timing on these is variable, so there's no guarantee exactly when it will happen.

▸ This means you'd need to book your XYZ for September, between May (or whenever the grid is available) and August 8.

▸ Call your knowledgeable II rep every once in awhile to see if the grid is out yet. As soon as it is published, check with them if Scottsdale is available in September.

▸ If Scottsdale in September is on the grid, book it as soon as you can. If Scottsdale is not possible, the rep can tell you what your other options are.

Expert tip: XYZ is shrinking. XYZ inventory has gone down in the past year or two, and it appears that since the recession is fading away and timeshare business has picked back up again, Interval has fewer units available to distribute via XYZ exchanges. If you want to try this out, I'd recommend doing it as soon as you can, because at some point this program of nearly-free weeks could shrink further, or disappear entirely.

Club Interval Points

Interval has its own points system, called Club Interval Gold, that uses Club Interval Points. While not as common as RCI Points, you may own a timeshare that's part of this system, or have an opportunity to join. Here's how it works.

Only certain resorts participate. You can't join this points program unless you own a week at a resort that has decided to be part of the Club Interval program. If you do own at such a resort, then you may decide to add your timeshare week to this optional program (for a price, of course).

Deposit your week, get II points. If your timeshare is part of this program, when you deposit your week with II, you get a certain number of Club Interval Points placed in your account. You then use these points to book vacations.

No separate inventory. Unlike RCI points, there is not a separate inventory for II weeks vs. II points. You have access to the same selection of vacation inventory either way.

It's all about the grid. Interval International publishes a table for Club Interval Weekly Points Values, and this is the key to this system. This grid determines how many points you get when you deposit your week, and it also determines how many points it costs you to book a vacation. Here's a snippet of the table to show how it works. (The actual table is much larger.)

TDI Range	2-Bedroom	1-Bedroom
135-150	78,750 - 105,000	67,500 - 90,000
115-130	65,625 - 87,500	56,250 - 75,000
90-110	52,500 - 70,000	45,000 - 60,000

Factors that determine your points. As you can see, two major factors that determine your points are your unit size and the TDI (Travel Demand Index) for the week you're depositing. That narrows it down to a range, for instance 65,625 to 87,500 if you're depositing a 2-bedroom in a week with TDI 115-130. Within that range, your specific points will vary based on the quality of resort accommodations you're depositing.

Deposit sooner to get more points. If you deposit at least 120 days in advance of the start of your week, you will get the full amount of points that your week is worth. As you get closer to the start date of your week, depositing it will get you fewer and fewer points. You cannot deposit your timeshare less than 2 weeks before the start date.

The same grid controls what you spend. When you want to book a vacation, the number of points required will be based on the same table. Short stays of 1 to 6 nights are based on a percentage of the weekly values, with Friday and Saturday nights costing the most.

Book multiple vacations. You can book as many vacations as you have points for. If you want to book a timeshare comparable in size, season, and quality to the week you own, that will probably be one. On the other hand, if you want to book smaller units, off-season stays, or short stay vacations, then you could end up with multiple vacations from your deposit of a single week.

Points last 2 years, no extensions. Your Club Interval Points are good for 2 years from the date of the week you deposited. This is the same time period you'd have if you deposited a normal week. The difference is that you can extend weeks, but you cannot extend points.

Learn more: All about II points. If you are considering joining Interval's points system, or are already part of it, you can find out more details in *All About Interval International Points*, at *TimeshareGame.com/owners-guide-links/*

Other opportunities with II

Short stay exchanges. Do you find it difficult to travel a week at a time? The short stay program might help with that. This lets Interval members book shorter vacations, from 1 to 6 nights, even if they're not part of the points program. Here's how it works.

▸ You must be a gold or platinum member with Interval in order to book a short stay exchange.

▸ If you own a week that's deposited with II, you can split it into two separate stays. If you own points, then you can book as many short stays as your points will cover.

▸ If you book a short stay using a full week deposit, then the other half of your deposited week stays in your account and you can use it for another short stay exchange.

▸ The inventory for short stays is usually short notice, though there may be exceptions.

▸ There are no pending exchange requests for short stays - you need to search and book them manually. You cannot use a bonus week AC to book a short stay.

Gold or platinum membership. These are premium memberships that provide additional services in exchange for a higher annual fee. Here's what you get and what it costs.

* **Additional benefits of Gold membership**: Short stay exchange abilities, $25 discount off the cost of Getaway vacations, Interval Options (which lets you exchange your timeshare towards a cruise, tour, golf or spa vacation), concierge service, and discount coupons for selected hotels, restaurants and other businesses.

* **Additional benefits of Platinum membership**: You get everything from gold level, but the Getaway discount is raised to $50. Platinum also includes free guest certificates, advance viewing of Getaway inventory, companion airline travel, special platinum escapes, and discounted airport lounge visits.

* **Upgrade fees**. The current fees to upgrade your membership are: Gold membership = $59/year (in addition to the normal yearly membership), Platinum membership = $129/year. (*All fees are subject to change.*)

E-Plus retrade protection. Sometimes you may want to retrade your exchange for something else, either due to a change in circumstances, or because you found something better. E-Plus is an Interval program that gives you this ability for a fee much lower than another exchange fee. Here's how it works.

▸ You purchase E-Plus as an add-on for an individual exchange transaction that you want to cover.

▸ This gives you the ability to retrade that exchange up to 3 times, requesting different resorts and/or different dates, with no additional fee.

▸ You can purchase E-Plus when you set up a pending exchange request, or at any time up to 5 days after your exchange is confirmed. After the 5-day period is over, you lose your ability to get E-Plus for that exchange.

▸ The current fee for E-Plus is $49.

Guest certificates. You can give someone a vacation that you booked on Interval International by purchasing a guest certificate. This will change the reservation from your name to theirs. Unless you're a platinum member with II, you must pay a $49 fee for this.

Tips for planning your II exchanges

Plan around company preferences. In II, the company preferences for Marriott and Starwood make a major difference, especially for the most popular locations and seasons. If you don't have this company preference, then you really can't count on getting one of these vacations. There's always a chance that you might get lucky and snag a late cancellation, but it's not likely. If you want to book a popular destination and season, it's wise to include some resorts in your exchange request that aren't subject to the company preference.

Use your top deposits for the most difficult exchange requests. Though II doesn't show you the trading power of your deposits, if you have more than one timeshare on deposit, you probably have a good idea of their relative values. If you're going to run more than one pending exchange request, make sure to use your most valuable deposit to request the most difficult timeshare. You could make an exception in case of unit size requirements or expiration dates, but in general, using your top deposit for the hardest request is most likely to yield the match you're looking for.

Expert tip: Get easy exchanges with an XYZ if possible. Keep in mind that you can get an XYZ 2-for-1 exchange with every regular week exchange that you make. They're fairly short notice and the availability is quite limited, but in general you can use an XYZ for off-season travel to locations that have plenty of timeshare inventory. (For details on how XYZ exchanges work, see *Getting extra weeks with II*.)

If you are thinking of any shoulder or low season trips, check into whether you could use an XYZ to book that vacation, rather than using a regular exchange. This would give you the low season trip for just an exchange fee, and let you save your normal timeshare deposit for something that is harder to book.

For instance, say you're thinking of going to Las Vegas in September. Could you make the timing work for that as an XYZ? If you have a regular exchange in July, a September trip to Vegas might work within the XYZ time limits.

If the timing is possible, then is this on the XYZ grid? Even if the grid isn't yet available, an II rep can probably tell you whether Las Vegas has been available for September in the past, especially if you have found an XYZ knowledgeable rep to work with. If Vegas is on the grid for September, then you just got an almost free vacation!

This trick won't always work, but when it does, it lets you maximize the use of your valuable timeshare, rather than spending it on something you could get with an XYZ.

Worksheet E - Tracking II Exchanges

Summary

II gives you the ability to exchange your timeshare for many different resorts around the world. You'll get the best exchanges if you know how to work the system, and stay on top of your timeshare exchange activities.

This worksheet is for tracking your deposits and exchanges that go through Interval International. You can also use it for any other exchange company besides RCI. (RCI has a very different system and a separate worksheet.)

How to use this worksheet

- **Sections by timeshare year** - Down the left side, you have groups of rows separated into years, based on the check-in date of the timeshare week you deposit. You'll have activities related to this week in different years, but keep everything for this week tracked in its original year.

- **Weeks deposited** - Whenever you deposit a timeshare into II, enter the deposit on the left side, along with details like the timeshare and unit type, the Exchange # (a tracking number used in II), the date you made the deposit, and the expiration date of that deposit.

  Expert tip: Tracking XYZ opportunities.
  Whenever you deposit a week into II, create another row below it for the XYZ that you can get with that deposit. This helps you remember that you have these available, so that you can maximize your use of them.

- **Bonus weeks are treated like a deposit** - When you get an Accommodation Certificate (bonus week) from II, enter it as another deposit on the worksheet. This is another exchange opportunity for you to track and make use of.

- **Deposits and exchanges on the same row** - Each deposit, bonus week AC, or XYZ, is entered on its own row, on the left side. When you use that deposit, AC or XYZ for an exchange, the exchange goes into the right side, on the same row. This way you can easily see how all of your deposits and exchange opportunities were used.

- **Instant exchanges** - If you do an instant exchange online or over the phone, enter the exchange details on the right side of the spreadsheet, next to the deposit you used for the exchange. Enter details like the resort, unit size, check-in date and confirmation date.

- **Pending exchange requests** - When you set up a pending exchange request, enter the details of it on the right side of the spreadsheet, next to the deposit you are using for that search. You can also color code them together so that it's easy to see which deposits are tied up with which searches. Enter details like the location, unit size, and dates you are searching for, as well as the date you started the search.

• **Deposit first exchanges** - In this case, you have the deposit entered in the worksheet as soon as you make the deposit to II. You then enter the details about your exchange request next to this deposit when you start the search. Put Exchange Type = "Dep first."

• **Request first exchanges** - In this case, you are starting the search before you make a deposit to II, but you still need to know what timeshare you expect to use for the exchange. Enter the details of your search, along with the basic info for the timeshare you plan to use. Put Exchange Type = "Req first."

• **Search modifications** - If you modify your search later on, enter another row for the modified search, with notes about what you changed, and when you changed it. This is helpful so you can see the history of what happened.

• **Vacations reserved and completed** - When you get an exchange, enter the details about it here, including the resort, unit size, check-in date, and confirmation date. If you were using a Request first exchange, also enter the details for the timeshare you are exchanging. Color coding shows which vacations you have coming up, and which you have already taken.

• **Open deposits** - You can have multiple open deposits at one time, and these can include XYZ or bonus weeks that you have available for exchange. It's good to highlight these in yellow, since these are what you have to work with right now. Be sure to watch the expiration dates, so that nothing goes to waste.

• **Fees paid** - Whenever you pay Interval a fee for a transaction, enter the amount and date next to that exchange.

- **Dates to watch** - If you have certain dates you need to pay attention to, note them on here and highlight them. Examples could include:

  ▸ Deposits which have an expiration date

  ▸ Dates when you can use an XYZ exchange

  ▸ Pending requests that are approaching your desired trip date (so you can make alternate plans if needed)

  ▸ Reminders to deposit a week at the right time to maximize your trading power.

Usage tips

- **Stay up to date** - Review this at regular intervals (perhaps monthly), and keep it up to date. This helps you stay on top of what you have available, how your requests are progressing, and any critical dates that you need to watch out for.

- **Multiple timeshares** - If you have multiple timeshares in II, track them all together on this spreadsheet. RCI exchanges have a different worksheet.

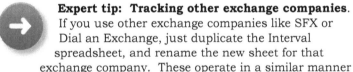 **Expert tip: Tracking other exchange companies**. If you use other exchange companies like SFX or Dial an Exchange, just duplicate the Interval spreadsheet, and rename the new sheet for that exchange company. These operate in a similar manner to the way that II works, so starting with the II spreadsheet works well.

Links to worksheets

- SAMPLE worksheet - This copy is filled out with sample data for different types of timeshares. The data is not real - it's purely for illustration purposes, so you can see how the spreadsheet works.

- BLANK worksheet - For your own use.

- Worksheets are at
  TimeshareGame.com/owners-guide-links/

9. Option C - Multiplying Your Vacations

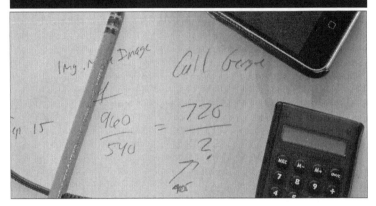

Getting extra exchanges for your timeshare

Want more vacations? Depending on what exchange company you go through, there are ways that you can get multiple exchanges from your timeshare. Here are some possibilities.

RCI: Work the TPU differences

You can often multiply your vacations by maximizing the trading power of your deposit, then using those TPUs to book multiple vacations that cost you less trading power. For example, you might get 40 TPUs for depositing your timeshare, and use that to book 5 vacation weeks that each cost 8 TPUs.

☑️ **Maximize your deposit**. Make sure your deposit gets you as much trading power as possible, following the tips in _Maximizing your RCI trading power_. This is something you always want to plan when you're exchanging, so that you can get as much value from your timeshare as possible.

☑️ **Look for bargain exchanges** that cost a fraction of the TPUs you received for your deposit. This can be a combination of short notice exchanges, special sales, off-season visits, or smaller units. Short notice exchanges can often yield some cool bargains, and RCI sometimes has exchange sales where weeks are available for as little as 4 or 5 TPUs.

☑️ **You can do a similar thing with RCI points**. You don't have a choice about maximizing your own points, but you can still look for bargain vacations that use up fewer points, so you can get more vacation days.

Interval: Use XYZs and bonus weeks

These two programs from Interval International can give you additional vacations for minimal costs. There are restrictions on both programs, but if you can travel to the selected destinations without a lot of lead time, these can be a great way to multiply your vacations.

☑ **Use XYZs for double vacations**. XYZ exchanges are a hidden program in II, that gives you 2-for-1 exchanges. It's not documented or publicized - you need to know about it and call to ask for it. There are significant limitations on what you can get with an XYZ exchange, but when it works out, it's pretty sweet. You get an extra vacation week for just the cost of an exchange fee. For more about XYZs, see *Getting extra weeks with II*.

☑ **Watch for II bonus weeks**. II sometimes offers a bonus week (also called an Accommodation Certificate or AC for short), as an incentive. For instance, you might get an AC if you deposit your timeshare by a certain date, or if you book a Getaway during a certain promotion. The AC gives you an extra vacation week you can use for selected destinations for a nominal fee. For more about ACs, see *Getting extra weeks with II*.

Other exchange companies: Watch the promotions

If you want to use one of the smaller exchange companies, then watch their promotions and time your deposit with them accordingly. You may see a special offer like "Deposit your week by February 1 and get 2 bonus weeks." That's a nice deal, giving you two extra vacation weeks, on top of your exchange.

The bonus weeks you get on a deal like this typically have restrictions on how you can use them, and specifics will vary for different companies and offers. You may be limited to fairly short-notice travel for the bonus weeks. Usually you just need to pay the exchange fee to make use of one. If you're going to use one of the independent exchange companies, these are a potential source of nearly free vacations.

Splitting your unit for double the fun

Most timeshares are resort condos, with studio, 1-bedroom, and 2-bedroom units being the most common sizes. If you own a week in a 2, 3 or 4-bedroom unit, find out whether you can split your unit. When a unit is splittable, it's called a "lock-off" or "lock-out." This can be a great advantage.

How a lock-off works. Lock-off units have a locking door that can split the unit in two. For instance, a 2-bedroom lock-off might be split into a 1-bedroom plus a studio. A 3-bedroom lock-off might be split into a 2-bedroom plus a 1-bedroom.

Each of the smaller units has its own separate keyed entrance, so they can be used independently. The smaller locked-off units each have their own beds, baths, living areas and kitchen facilities, though often one of the units gets the main kitchen and living room, while the smaller side of the lock-off could have limited kitchen facilities.

Using the entire unit together. If you're using the entire timeshare unit together, then you'll have the separating door unlocked. Members of your family can come and go between the two sides, since it's all one big unit.

Using the lock-off sides separately. If the two smaller units are being used independently, the door between will stay locked. The resort will book each of the smaller units to different people. Guest on both sides come and go through their own entrances, and it's just as if the connecting door was a solid wall.

Flexibility of owning a lock-off. Why is owning a lock-off a good thing? Because it gives you many more options for how to use your timeshare week. For example, if you owned a 2BR lock-off that splits into a 1BR + Studio, here are a few ways you could work with it.

✳   You could use the full 2BR unit for a week with your family.

✱ You could use a 1BR unit one week, plus a studio a different week, for 2 weeks of vacation at your resort.

✱ You could invite friends or relatives for a vacation. They'd get the studio, and you'd get the 1BR. You could get together for group meals and activities, but the rest of the time, you'd have sufficient separate facilities to stay out of each other's hair.

✱ You could use the studio week at your home resort, and trade the 1BR for a week somewhere else.

✱ You could use the 1BR at your home resort, and rent out the studio to help offset your maintenance fees.

As you can see, the ability to lock off your timeshare gives you far more flexibility than you'd have otherwise.

Watch out: There may be lock-off costs. You may have to pay an additional fee to divide your unit, which falls into that unfortunate category of "fees for anything we can think of." In spite of the fee, though, this can be well worthwhile. You can get an extra vacation week for just the cost of a lock-off transaction, with no additional maintenance fees.

Lock-off units in weeks vs. points. The concept of lock-offs works differently if you own weeks vs. points.

● **Weeks**. If you own a week in a lock-off unit, then you can split it up and use, exchange, or rent the two sides as discussed. The two smaller units would both be for the season you own (high / mid / low).

● **Points**. If you own points equivalent to a week in the same 2BR lock-off unit, then you could use your points for a 1BR week + a studio week, but you'd have other options, too. For instance, those points might get you 3 weeks in a studio in a lower season.

Watch out: Fixed week lock-offs. If you own a fixed week lock-off, then you would not be able to book two separate vacations with it at your home resort, since both sides of your lock-off would be for the exact same week. However, you could still use one side yourself and deposit the other for exchange, possibly even exchanging back into your own resort at another time if that's what you want.

Expert tip: With RCI, lock-offs can increase your trading power. If you own a week in a lock-off unit, you can usually get significantly more trading power in RCI if you split your unit in two, deposit the pieces separately into RCI, then combine your deposits. There are fees to do this (of course), but it can make an enormous difference.

Here's an example:

▸ Deposit full 2-bedroom together = 24 TPUs

▸ Deposit 1-bedroom side of lock-off = 21 TPUs

▸ Deposit studio side of lock-off = 19 TPUs

▸ Combine the deposits from two lock-offs = 21 + 19 = 40 TPUs

Locking off and depositing separately would give you 40 TPUs to use instead of just 24. You'd have almost double the trading power available, which could get you either more vacations or a more valuable vacation.

Expert tip: With II, lock-offs could quadruple your vacations. If you're a member of Interval International and you own a lock-off, then you may be able to do even better than doubling your vacations. If you can make use of XYZ exchanges, you can (a) split your lock-off into two pieces, (b) deposit both sides with II, (c) get two exchange vacations for your two deposits, and (d) get two XYZ exchanges for your two normal exchanges.

This would give you 4 weeks of vacation from your 1 timeshare week. For more on XYZs, see *Getting extra weeks with II*.

Taking short stay vacations

For many people with work and/or school schedules to consider, it's hard to take week long vacations. Shorter trips can work well to maximize your vacations when you have a busy schedule. The traditional timeshare weeks model didn't lend itself to this, but there are more ways to work the system than there used to be. Here are a few tips.

Points owners can choose their length. If you are a points owner, then you aren't tied to full week stays, and can take shorter trips instead. This is one of the biggest advantages to owning timeshare points. It's easy to plan long weekends or other short getaways spaced throughout the year.

Rules can make getting shorter stays more difficult. Some companies have reservation restrictions that give preference to people booking longer stays. For instance, if you own Wyndham points, then you could book a 3, 4 or 7-night vacation up to 10 months in advance, but could only book a 2-night vacation up to 3 months in advance during prime season. A lot of desirable inventory will be gone by that time.

Interval offers short stays for weeks owners. If you own a timeshare week, you can get short stay vacations without converting to points, if you are a member of Interval International. If you upgrade your II membership to Gold or Platinum, then you can deposit one timeshare week with II and use that to get two short stay vacations. See *Other opportunities with II* for more details.

Short stays are most economical close to home. Short stays are most advantageous if you're staying somewhere fairly close to home, since otherwise transportation costs and travel time can add up. If you pay $650 in airfare for a week of vacation, that's more reasonable on a per-night basis than doing the same for a weekend getaway. On the other hand, if it's just a couple of hours drive to your destination, the travel cost and time are not an issue.

Fees can add up for short stays. Booking multiple short stays usually means paying more fees than if you booked one full week vacation. The more short stays you book, the more expensive this gets. Of course, you also get more separate trips this way, so it's often well worth the fees.

Here's an example showing how this could work in RCI Points:
▸ Book one 7-night stay = $169 reservation fee

▸ Book a 3-night stay + a 4-night stay = $89 + $109 = $198

▸ Book three 2-night stays + a 1-night stay = 3 * $69 + $49 = $256

> **Expert tip: Fit shorter stays around your main vacation**. If you're a points owner, it can often work well to book a couple of nights at a different location before and/or after your main vacation. For example, if you are driving to Breckenridge for a week long timeshare vacation, you could break up the trip and make the drive more fun by booking a couple of nights at a different resort along the way.

Extra, Getaway, and Last Call vacations

RCI, Interval International and some of the other exchange companies, let you buy additional vacation time at selected resorts. These are vacations that don't require you to exchange anything, you just pay for it directly. The only requirement is that you must be a member of that exchange company.

Access to these vacation opportunities is a significant benefit of timeshare ownership. Here's how they work.

Multiply your vacations. These programs give you a great way to multiply your vacation time. Some timeshare owners end up spending more time in these extra vacations than they do in their own timeshares. It's perfectly possible to own one week at a resort somewhere, and use your exchange company membership to buy 5 or 10 value priced additional weeks at different resorts all over. There's no set limit to how many you can purchase.

Bargain vacations. Sometimes you'll find exceptional deals, like a 1-bedroom ski week for $199 - less than $30/night! There are sometimes bargains available like this that you just can't touch with hotels. Of course, prices vary tremendously and you will also see weeks that cost thousands of dollars. There are great deals out there, however, especially for off season or shoulder season travel.

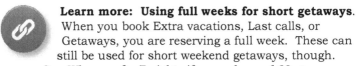 **Learn more: Using full weeks for short getaways**. When you book Extra vacations, Last calls, or Getaways, you are reserving a full week. These can still be used for short weekend getaways, though. See *Why pay for 7 nights if you only need 2?* at *TimeshareGame.com/owners-guide-links/*

Extra Vacations (RCI). RCI makes 7-night stays at various resorts available as Extra Vacations. There's no depositing a timeshare week or points, you just pay with your credit card when you make the reservation. You can choose from hundreds of resorts, and prices vary widely. You can book as many Extra Vacations as you want.

Getaways (Interval International). Interval's name for the same type of program is Getaways. They offer week-long stays at many resorts, and you pay for these vacations directly, rather than exchanging your own timeshare. You can book up to one year in advance, and prices vary considerably. Interval International reserves the right to limit your number of Getaways, but it's unlikely that you'll run into problems unless they think you're abusing the system.

Last Call Vacations (RCI). These are short notice vacation weeks, available less than 45 days before check-in. If your lifestyle lets you travel without much lead time, these are all bargain priced vacations. The prices are fixed based on the unit size. It currently ranges from $244 for a week in a studio, up to $309 for a 2-bedroom (all prices subject to change). This means you're always paying less than $45 per night, even for a 2-bedroom timeshare unit.

Expert tip: Extra Vacations can beat Last Calls. Sometimes you can find an Extra Vacation that's even cheaper than the bargain prices on Last Call vacations. Last Calls follow a fixed schedule for cost by unit type, while prices on Extra Vacations can vary. There are times when an off-season 1-bedroom on an Extra Vacation can be as low as $199, compared to a Last Call price of $269. Always check your options.

Finding what's available. You can go online anytime, and browse through the selection of these additional vacations to see what's available. You cannot enter an on-going search or pending request for these - you have to find them yourself with manual searching. It's fun to look around, and discover all the places you can go.

Keep checking. It's good to keep checking now and then to get a feel for what's out there, and what the prices look like. Prices and selection will vary with season, demand, and inventory. The more you watch it, the more you'll learn what you can expect. If there's a particular destination you're interested in, you'll see which resorts tend to have availability, and what the normal price range is.

Watch for the sales. You can find outstanding deals when a company decides to have a special sale. Sometimes you'll get an e-mail message alerting you to a sale opportunity. Other times you won't be notified, but if you log onto your RCI or II account, you may see something like "2-days only! Sale on Getaways." Selection will dwindle over the course of the sale, so the sooner you look, the more you can find.

Expert tip: Planning around the deals. There are two approaches to vacation planning. The most common is to decide where you want to go, and then see what you can get for that location. An alternative is to watch the deals, and when you see something that looks great, plan your vacation based on the deal. You may end up going somewhere you never thought of, just because they had an incredible offer on it.

Watch out: Read the fine print and watch for fees. Sometimes there may be add-on fees on top of your discount vacation that change the equation completely. One particularly egregious example is the "All inclusive fee," charged by some resorts. Here's how it works. You buy a 7-night extra vacation for $209, thinking you have a great deal at a Caribbean resort. However, the fine print says you have to pay a mandatory "All inclusive fee" of $925 per person, payable at check-in. All of a sudden, the cost went from $209 to $2,059. Yikes!

Learn more: Pros and cons of all-inclusive vacations. See how these fees work out in real life, with an analysis of the pros and cons. Sometimes all-inclusive makes sense, but other times it really doesn't. See *All-inclusive fees can multiply your costs* at *TimeshareGame.com/owners-guide-links/*

No renting these out. Both RCI and II expressly prohibit you from purchasing one of these additional vacation weeks then renting it out. If they catch you doing this, you could lose the money you paid, have your account suspended, or face other sanctions.

Bonus time and day use

What is bonus time? Some resorts let owners rent extra nights (bonus time) at a discount rate when space is available.

Not every timeshare offers bonus time, but when yours does, this can be a nice benefit.

How bonus time works. When a timeshare resort has units unbooked a short time in advance, they may make these available to owners for a preferential rate. This bonus time is totally separate from your normal timeshare use - it's just renting extra vacation time at your resort.

Rules vary. Like most things about timeshares, the rules vary from company to company. Check with your own timeshare. Here are some questions to ask.

▸ **Do they have bonus time?** Some companies do, some don't, and some have it only at certain resorts.

▸ **Where can you use it?** Can you get bonus time at your home resort only, or at other resorts in the group?

▸ **When can you book it?** Bonus time is usually intended to fill last-minute units that might otherwise go empty. Often bonus time opens for booking 14 or 21 days in advance.

▸ **Who can use it?** Some companies allow only owners to use bonus time, while others allow guests to use bonus time as well. Guest bookings may have an even shorter lead time than owner bookings.

▸ **How long can you stay?** There may be a minimum or maximum stay. For instance, there could be a 2 night minimum on weekends, 1 night minimum other times, and a 3 night maximum anytime.

▸ **Whats the cost?** You may find that the cost is tied to the maintenance fees, or there could be a different pricing structure.

Don't count on this for peak reservations. Since bonus time sells inventory that's available on short notice, being able to use it relies on having space available. It may not be available at popular resorts, during prime seasons, or on weekends.

Last minute cancellations can open up. If there's nothing available 14 days in advance, you can try again closer to the date you want to arrive. Occasionally, last minute cancellations will open up a space.

Watch out: Compare prices with other sources. Some timeshare owners have been dismayed to find units at their own timeshare resort available for rent to the public on a site like Hotels.com, for less than their cost to rent straight from the resort as owners with bonus time. Just because bonus time is touted as a benefit of ownership doesn't mean it's always the best deal. Shop around and see what you find.

Timeshares with day use. Some resorts offer their owners day use privileges. As an owner there, you are allowed to stop in and use the pool, grounds, or other facilities on a day use basis, even when you are not staying at the resort. Check with your own timeshare to see if this is offered.

Day use is best for nearby owners. Obviously, day use privileges have the most value when you're able to stop in and make use of them without a lot of added cost. Having a day use resort an hour's drive from your home is more likely to be useful than one that takes expensive airfare to get there.

Renting someone else's timeshare

You don't always need to own a timeshare to stay there. There are many timeshares available to rent. This can be a good way to enjoy a timeshare vacation without the commitment and on-going costs of ownership. There are different approaches to renting.

Rent from the company. Many timeshare companies and resorts have a website where you can rent units directly from the company. This is different from bonus time described earlier, in that you don't need to be an owner - these rentals are open to the general public. If there's a resort where you're interested in staying, check it out online and see if they have rentals available.

Rent through an online travel site. Many timeshare companies rent open inventory to the public through travel sites like Orbitz or Travelocity. It's worth comparing the prices between sites, to see whether these third-party sites have better prices than renting directly from the resort.

Rent from another owner. Some timeshare owners rent their weeks out to other people. The way it works is that they make a reservation and get a guest certificate in your name. You pay the owner the agreed rental amount, and show up for your vacation using the guest certificate to check in.

Renting points instead of weeks. If you own timeshare points, you may be able to rent points either from the company or directly from another owner in the same system, giving you a one-time use of those points. Whether you can do this will depend on the rules for your company, but it can be a good way to augment your own points to get you more or better vacations than you could otherwise get.

Where to find rentals by owner. There are numerous sites where people can advertise their timeshares for rent. Here are a few of the most popular.

▸ Redweek.com -- This site has extensive listings of timeshares for rent direct from the owner.

▸ TUG (tug2.net) -- The timeshare user's group (TUG) has a classified ads section with many timeshares available to rent from owners.

▸ eBay -- You can find almost anything on eBay, and timeshare rentals are no exception.

Watch out: Verify the reservation before you pay. Unfortunately, there are scammers in the world who can claim to make a reservation for you, take your money, and leave you with nothing. Call the resort to verify the reservation in your name before you pay. Also, using a credit card for payment gives you an avenue to dispute the charge in case there is a problem.

Expert tip: Renting as an alternative to exchanging. Some people use renting as an exchange method. They rent out their own timeshare, then rent a different timeshare from someone else. Some advantages of this method are that there is no exchange fee, and you're not limited by your trading power - you can book anything you want to pay for. A disadvantage of this approach is that it takes more work on your part than going through an exchange company. See the section on *Renting out your timeshare*.

Expert tip: Renting can get you peak weeks. Let's say you want to visit a popular Caribbean resort over Christmas week. Your chances of getting this on an exchange are slim to none, and such prime units are rarely open for booking on websites either. Owners who paid peak prices for these prime timeshare weeks want to use their ownership themselves, or rent it out instead. Many realize a tidy profit year after year by renting their unit, which makes this a possible avenue for you to book what you want. If you're looking for a high-demand week, check the rental listings. It may not be cheap, but it could get you the vacation you want.

Watch out: Renting can cost more than other approaches. Of course timeshare owners would love to cover their maintenance fees and make a profit by renting their timeshares. That's natural as a goal, but it's not always realistic, especially in off-peak seasons. If you're looking for a vacation where there's decent availability, compare rental prices against the cost of using a timeshare exchange, or booking an extra vacation from RCI or II. Sometimes people ask rental prices that are too steep to compete.

10. Option D - Taking Fewer Vacations

Sometimes life gets in the way of vacations, and you can't use your timeshare one year. That doesn't mean it needs to go to waste, though.

There are ways you can still get some benefit from your timeshare now, or save it for future use when you have more time available. The important thing is to plan ahead, so that the timeshare you're paying for doesn't vanish, leaving you with bills and no benefit. What a waste that would be!

Extending your timeshare's usability

Depending on what you own and what companies you work with, there are various ways you can save your timeshare week or points to use in a future year. As always, different systems have different rules, and it's important to learn what your options are with your timeshare.

There are a couple of avenues you can use to approach this.

- **Your own timeshare company**. If you own timeshare points, your timeshare company has rules about how you can extend the life of your points. See the table below for an overview of how this works.

- **Timeshare exchange companies**. Whether you own weeks or points, you can often extend the life of your timeshare by using the exchange companies, and knowing how their deposit rules and expiration dates work. The second table below discusses this further.

Extending with your timeshare company

Here is an overview of what you can do to extend the life of your points with some of the major timeshare companies in the US.

Company	Extending the life of your points
Bluegreen Vacation Club (BVC)	Points expire at the end of the use year, but can be saved for a second year, with restricted usage. After 2 years, they are gone.
Diamond Resorts International (DRI)	Points expire at the end of the use year. You can save them for one additional year, as follows: save up to 100% of points by June 30, 50% of points by Aug 31, 25% of points by Oct 31.
Disney Vacation Club (DVC)	Points are good for one year, but can be saved (banked) for a second year for no charge.
Hilton Grand Vacation Club (HGVC)	Points expire at the end of the calendar year. You can deposit next year's points to extend them one year, or rescue this year's points to extend them one year with some restrictions.
Marriott Vacation Club (MVC)	Points expire at the end of the use year. You can save (bank) them one additional year, if you do so at least 6 months prior to the original expiration date.
RCI Points	RCI points expire at the end of their use year, but are saved automatically for a 2nd year. You can extend them for a 3rd, and after three years, they're gone.
Starwood Vacation Ownership (SVO)	Staroptions expire at the end of the use year. You can extend them (roll them over) for one more year.
Vacation Resorts International (VRI)	There are no VRI points. Some VRI weeks may be part of RCI Points.

Company	Extending the life of your points
Westgate Resorts	Westgate uses weeks, not points.
Worldmark, The Club	Credits you don't use during their year will automatically carry over to the following year, and expire at the end of that year.
Wyndham (Club Wyndham)	Points expire at the end of the use year. Before the start of the use year, you can pool your points, making them available for 3 years.

Expert tip: Know your deadline dates. If you own points and want to save or extend them, make sure you know the deadline. If you miss the deadline to save your points, you could lose them entirely. For example, with Bluegreen points, you must elect to save them before their original expiration date. With Diamond points, if you waited until the expiration date, you would have lost your chance to save them. Don't let your points go to waste by missing a deadline.

Extending with an exchange company

Whether you own a timeshare week or points, there are often ways that you can extend the usable life of your timeshare by depositing it with an exchange company. Here's an overview of the most popular exchange companies and how you can use them to extend your timeshare, rather than letting it expire.

Company	How it works
RCI Weeks	Deposited weeks are good for up to 2 years from the check-in date of the deposited week. You can extend this up to 1 more year for a fee, or extend indefinitely by combining deposits judiciously.
RCI Points	RCI points expire at the end of their use year, but are saved automatically for a 2nd year. You can extend them for a 3rd, and after three years, they're gone.
II Weeks	Deposited weeks are good for up to 2 years from the check-in date on the deposited week. You can extend this up to 1 year for a fee, with limited capabilities.
II Points	Club Interval Points expire 2 years from the check-in date of the underlying week deposited. You cannot extend them.
VRI*ety exchange	Weeks deposited with VRI*ety expire 2 years after the check-in date. This can be extended for a fee.
Dial an Exchange	You can deposit a week or a week's worth of points, and receive an exchange credit good for 3 years.

Expert tip: Don't wait until the last minute. If you're going to deposit your timeshare into an exchange company, deposit it as soon as you know you won't be using it yourself, so you can get the maximum trading power. If you wait until close to your check-in date to deposit it, you can lose a lot of its value.

Saving up for a special vacation

Side benefit of saving can be a better vacation. Extending your unused timeshare from one year to the next can often have a side benefit. Along with the primary goal of getting value from the timeshare you've paid for but couldn't use, this may also let you save your points or trading power for a larger vacation the next year.

Planning for a bigger unit or pricier resort. Perhaps you've got your eye on one of the Disney resorts that normally costs more in a trade than what you own. Or perhaps you'd like to take the extended family on a vacation, requiring a larger unit or two separate units. You might even want to take a Caribbean vacation, and spend a week on each of two different islands. In these situations, you may be able to "save up" to get the vacation you want.

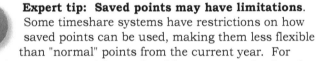 **Expert tip: Saved points may have limitations**. Some timeshare systems have restrictions on how saved points can be used, making them less flexible than "normal" points from the current year. For instance, you might not be able to use saved points for peak season reservations, or might only be able to make reservations with them 6 months in advance. When you're planning to save points for a special vacation, make sure the rules for your timeshare won't throw a wrench into your plans.

Borrow and save together for even more. When you want a lot of points for your super vacation, you may be able to get triple points by borrowing and saving at the same time. For example, say you want to take a big European vacation in 2017. With most companies, you could save your 2016 points forward to 2017, and borrow your 2018 points in 2017 too. This would give you triple points you could use in 2017.

Combine TPUs in RCI weeks. If you own a week that's part of RCI, you can save your trading power and use it the next year. By combining your deposits in RCI, you can merge the trading power (TPUs) from your 2015 week, 2016 week, and as many other deposits as you like. This can give you a large deposit that's able to pull the hard-to-book exchange vacation you want.

You cannot combine weeks in II. Interval International doesn't give you a way to combine different weeks you deposit. If you've got both a 2015 week and a 2016 week deposited with II, you must use them for separate vacation exchanges. You could book consecutive exchange weeks to get a 2-week vacation, but you can't combine them to get a larger unit or more expensive resort.

Guest certificates and gifting a vacation

You can't use it, but can someone else? If circumstances mean that you cannot use your timeshare vacation this year, perhaps someone else could. Is there a close friend or family member who you'd like to give a vacation? This could make a most memorable gift.

Milestone birthdays or anniversaries. Perhaps it's your sister's 40th birthday, your son's honeymoon, or your parents' 50th wedding anniversary. Special occasions like this are an ideal time to give someone the gift of a vacation. Rather than using your own timeshare as normal, you can provide a wonderful gift. They're sure to enjoy it a lot more than a silver serving dish!

Employee rewards. Some timeshare owners who have their own businesses, give away vacations as rewards for exceptional employee performance. That could be a powerful incentive.

Guest certificates are the answer. To give a timeshare vacation as a gift, you just book your vacation as usual, then arrange for a guest certificate in your recipient's name. When they show up for the holiday, they bring the confirmation in their name, and matching identification. It's simple.

Guest certificates via your own resort. If you want to give somebody a vacation at your own timeshare, just reserve your vacation as normal, then call the company and arrange a guest certificate.

Guest certificates via an exchange company. You can also give away exchange vacations or resort stays you purchased as an extra vacation. You just need to purchase a guest certificate from RCI, II, or whatever other exchange company you are using.

Expert tip: Do you have frequent guests? RCI has a Guest Pass program that lets you buy a guest pass for one specific person that's good for five years. This means you don't need to pay the Guest Certificate fee for them each time you give them a vacation.

Transferring points to give a vacation. If your recipient has a timeshare account in the same points system as you do, this is an alternate way to give them the gift of a vacation. Rather than you making a reservation and buying a guest certificate, you could transfer a certain number of timeshare points to their account. They could then use these to book a vacation themselves. Not all timeshare points systems have this feature.

Using points for airlines, cars and more

Your points system may allow you to use your points to pay for airline tickets, hotel stays, car rentals, cruises, or more. Each different company has its own terminology and rules. Here are a few tips.

The flexibility can be nice. The big selling point of programs like this is flexibility. It gives you additional ways to use your points, beyond booking timeshare accommodation. If you have more points than you need for vacation stays, this can be useful.

There may be restrictions. Like other aspects of timesharing, companies have different rules about where and how you can use your points.   For instance, RCI allows you to use up to 33% of your annual points on Points Partners (their name for this program), and there are some RCI points resorts that are not eligible for the program at all.

There will be fees. This is no surprise. When you use your points to book a plane ticket, hotel, entertainment pass, or other non-timeshare product, you will have to pay a transaction fee in addition to surrendering your points. Fees vary by company and transaction.

Watch out: Using points may not be a good deal. It might seem like you're getting that plane ticket nearly free, but that's not really the case.
Remember that you paid money for those points, both for the initial purchase and the annual maintenance fees. Sometimes you will find that the cost of your points + the transaction fee is more than you would pay to buy the airline ticket directly. Always shop around for comparison prices before you use one of these deals.

Expert tip: This can be useful for points near expiration. One time it can make sense to use your points like this is when you have some points that are about to expire, with no further chance to extend them. If your points can buy you a hotel or car rental, even if it's not the best deal around, it's better than letting the points expire unused.

Watch out: Using points to pay maintenance fees. Some companies let you use points to pay your annual timeshare fees. This is not cost effective, as it's a sure bet that the amount you pay for the points is higher than the dollar value you get out of them by doing this. The only times it might make sense to do this are if (a) you have some points near expiration, or (b) you have an unfortunate short-term cash flow issue. If this is anything more than a one-time temporary crunch, you'd be better off financially without owning those points at all. When the only benefit you're getting is partial payment of your fees, it's a losing proposition.

Renting out your timeshare

Sometimes you can rent out your unit to a third party. This can be a good option to recoup some of your maintenance fees if you are unable to use your timeshare one year. The first step is to learn the rules about what's allowed and what's not.

Know the rental rules

Here's an overview of the standard rules on renting timeshares. Just like most things, the rules vary between companies and resorts. Be sure to check with your own timeshare for specifics.

Renting is usually allowed at your own timeshare. If you own a timeshare week, most resorts will allow you rent it out. Some resorts do prohibit this, while other systems allow you rent out your "home week" (the specific unit, season and week that you own), but not any other unit or week. If you use points to book a stay within your own vacation club (i.e. not going through an exchange company), then you are usually allowed to rent that out.

Renting points may be allowed. This means selling someone the one-time use of your points, rather than selling them your points permanently. The renter would need a membership in the same timeshare system as you, and you would transfer the points to their account, for a price. This is an alternative to booking a reservation with your points and then renting out that unit. The rules on renting points vary by company. In some timeshare systems this is allowed, while in other systems it is not. In RCI points, you're allowed to transfer points for free to another member, but not to take money for them.

Watch out: Commercial renting prohibitions.
Let's say you're able to rent your timeshare for a
profit, and decide to buy more points and turn it
into an income stream. You could be in trouble.
Some companies allow renting on a small scale, but
prohibit it as a commercial venture. Renting out a week or two
now and then would be OK, but ramping it up to make it a
business could get you shut down.

Renting is never allowed by exchange companies. If you
book a vacation through one of the major exchange companies,
RCI or Interval International, renting that unit is strictly
prohibited. This applies whether you got the unit via a
timeshare exchange, booked it with points, or purchased it as
a Getaway or Extra Vacation. Vacations you book through RCI
or II cannot be rented out.

 **Watch out: Renting an exchange could lose you
a bundle**. The big exchange companies do enforce
their no-rental rules, and if they find you in
violation, you could lose the timeshare you're trying
to rent, the money you paid, and even your exchange
company membership.

Guest certificates required. To rent out your timeshare, you
must buy a guest certificate. You use the guest certificate to
put the reservation in your renter's name. Be sure to include
this cost when you're working out the pricing calculations.

Who can rent. Many timeshares require a renter to be at least
21 years old. Find out up front if you need to enforce a
restriction like this when you are renting out your timeshare.

Approaches to renting

Renting through your resort. Some timeshares have a rental
program, where they will handle renting out your unused unit,
and give you a portion of the rent they receive. If your
company does this, it's an easy way to go, but you won't get as

much as if you rent it yourself. It's common for the company to take up to 40% of the rent as a commission. Also make sure you know what happens if they don't find a renter.

Renting out a fixed week. This is a straight forward situation. If you own a fixed unit and week, then you already know exactly what you're renting, and can advertise it accordingly.

Floating week - Book then rent. If you own a floating week, there are a couple of ways you can go. With the "book then rent" approach, you reserve the week you want, then rent out that week. Make sure to reserve a week you think will have a high demand. The advantage of this approach is that you know you have the selected week booked for sure.

Floating week - Rent then book. An alternative approach is to advertise a rental with open dates, then book the week with your timeshare after you find out what dates the renter wants. An advantage here is that you might meet the needs of more potential renters. The risk is that you may not be able to get those dates, and the deal could fall through. The longer you take to find a renter and set the dates, the less chance you have of booking the best weeks.

Points - Book then rent vacation. Let's say you own points in a timeshare system that lets you book a week in Hawaii. Using this approach, you would book your Hawaii week, then rent out that vacation. You'd advertise the rental based on whatever price you thought that week could command.

Points - Rent then book vacation. Continuing the previous example, in this approach, you would advertise that you could book any vacation up to X points and rent it out. A potential renter could ask for a vacation in Hawaii or any other destination in that system. You'd book what they requested and then rent it to them. In this case, you'd advertise the rental based on a price per point.

Points - Rent straight points. If your system allows you to rent points to another owner, you could advertise renting either a fixed or variable amount of points, at a certain price per point. The price per point could be variable based on the amount rented, with a lower price if they rent more points.

Setting a rental price

There are a number of factors to consider when you're deciding how much to ask for rent.

Maintenance fees. Obviously you'd love to have the rent cover your maintenance fees, and even make you a profit if possible. Realistically, the price you can get will depend on the market and competition.

Season and week. Higher demand time periods can command much higher rental rates. If you own a summer week in Hilton Head, you've got something in demand. If you have Christmas week in the Caribbean, that's even better. Unfortunately, off-season timeshares can be difficult to rent, and you're unlikely to cover your maintenance fees.

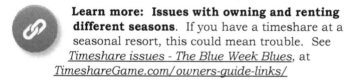 **Learn more: Issues with owning and renting different seasons**. If you have a timeshare at a seasonal resort, this could mean trouble. See *Timeshare issues - The Blue Week Blues*, at *TimeshareGame.com/owners-guide-links/*

Other costs. Include all your expected costs when you're working out the financial calculations. This could include guest certificate fees, payment processing fees, eBay fees, other advertising costs, or other fees from your timeshare company.

Competitive timeshare rentals. What are other rentals at the same time, in your same resort (or similar resorts) going for? Check eBay, Redweek, and TUG to find out what other people are asking. You can also check Expedia or Travelocity to see what they have listed for prices at your resort.

Timeframe. How quickly do you need to rent this? If you've got time to spare, then you can price it near the top of the

market. If you want to get a deal done quickly, then offering a
more attractive price can make it happen faster. As you get
closer to the date, you may need to lower the price.

Renting the timeshare

Decide your terms. Will you hold it for somebody without a
deposit? Do they need to give you full payment up front, or a
deposit up front and full payment later? Do you require a
damage deposit? When do you need to receive payment?
What about cancellation terms? You can decide the terms you
want. Looking at the terms competitive renters use can help
with your decision.

Decide how you will accept payment. Will you take payment
via Credit card? Personal check? Cashier's check? Electronic
transfer? Paypal? Money order? Many renters want the
convenience and security of paying with credit cards, so not
accepting these could limit your potential renters.

Watch out: Paypal rules on timeshare rentals.
PayPal rules specify that you cannot use their
service for any timeshare transactions, including
buying, selling, or renting timeshares. Some people
use it anyway for timeshare rentals, but this could lead
to a problem.

Escrow services. A renter may be understandably hesitant to
send a big check to somebody they don't know, many months
in advance of their vacation. To overcome this objection, you
can offer an escrow option like Deposit Guard*
(*depositguard.com*). In this case, a third party holds all of the
payments until after the rental. There is a service fee to do
this, but it may increase the renter's peace of mind. Decide up
front if you want to use escrow services or not. *This is not a
recommendation or endorsement of this particular company, it's
just an example.*

Prepare a rental agreement. You need to have a legal rental
agreement that you can give the renter to sign. You'll find

some examples on the TUG site (Timeshare Users Group).
Look those over, and make whatever changes you want in
order to come up with your own rental agreement.

Advertise your rental. You can list your timeshare rental
through one or more of the avenues below. You can also look
at free approaches, like posting it on your office bulletin board.
The more places you advertise it, the wider your potential
audience, but if you are paying to place ads, there's a tradeoff.

▸ eBay --   ebay.com

▸ Craigslist --   craigslist.com

▸ Redweek --   redweek.com

▸ Timeshare Users Group -- tug2.net

▸ Local newspapers (your own, or in likely target markets)

Watch out: Timeshare rental company scams.
Don't pay anybody an up front fee to rent your
timeshare for you, aside from a small charge to
place an ad. The normal result when you pay an up
front fee is nothing. You pay the fee, and they never
find a renter. You've lost your money, and your rental
opportunity too.

Rental process. The process you follow will depend on which
of the rental approaches discussed earlier you are using, as
well as the terms you decided on for your rental. Here's a
sample process, which you can tailor to your situation as
needed.

▸ Renter gives you a deposit to reserve the rental.

▸ You arrange the reservation with your resort, getting a
   guest certificate in the name of the renter.

▸ You send a copy of the reservation to the renter.

▸ The renter sends you the balance of the rental payment.

▸ You double check the reservation with the resort shortly
   before the check-in date.

▸ Renter stays at the timeshare, and has a wonderful time.

> **Watch out: Rental overpayment scams**. If the renter wants to send you extra money, this is a big red flag. One version of the scam is that he mistakenly sends you a check for more than the rent is, then says to go ahead and cash the check, and send him the difference. Another version is that he says he also needs to pay somebody else, so he wants to send you the combined amount, and have you pay the third party. Whether you pay the original "renter" or a third party, the result is the same. You send the money, their original check bounces, and you've lost your money.

11. Advanced Tactics & Evaluating Options

Using your own timeshare vs. exchanging

Pros and cons of using vs. exchanging

Sometimes the decision whether to use your own timeshare or exchange it for something else is a no-brainer. Perhaps you bought your timeshare at a place you love, and the family has a vacation tradition there every summer. Or perhaps you bought a timeshare specifically as a trader, with no intention of visiting your home resort.

Other times, the decision isn't as obvious. Here are some pros and cons of using vs. exchanging.

* **Pro: Using it may give you preferential booking**. In many systems, owners get advance booking over other people, and are able to snap up the most desirable reservations. If you want a high demand resort and season, this could give you the best odds of getting what you want. See _Chart - Weeks in different timeshare systems_ and _Chart - Using points in different systems_.

* **Pro: Using it gives you the option of renting**. When you book a vacation at your own timeshare, you usually have the option of renting it out to someone else. Once you deposit it with an exchange company, you lose that option. Even if you get an exchange back into the same resort, II and RCI rules prevent you from renting that out. For more, see the section _Renting out your timeshare_.

* **Pro: Using it minimizes your overall costs**. When you use your own timeshare, you avoid paying exchange fees. You may also be able to avoid paying an exchange company membership. Your total outlay for the year will normally be lower this way than if you go through RCI, II or one of the other exchange companies.

* **Con: Using it is not always the best deal**. Using your own timeshare does avoid exchange fees and give you a lower overall outlay. However, this may not be the best deal for staying at a particular resort. Sometimes there are great bargains available on exchanges, especially on short notice. See _Exchanging back to your own resort_.

* **Con: Exchanging gives you more flexibility**. The exchange companies open up your options to include thousands of vacation spots. Even if you own points in a major timeshare system, that system only includes a small percentage of the resorts available worldwide.

* **Con: Exchanging can give you more time**. Points systems have their own rules about whether and how you can extend your points, but if you own a timeshare week and let the year go by, your week is gone forever. Depositing it with an exchange company is a way to extend its life, so you can make use of it in the future. See _Extending your timeshare's usability_.

* **Con: Exchanging may let you multiply vacations**. If you have the free time available to take more than one week of vacation, then exchange companies can give you some options to do this. See the section _Getting extra exchanges for your timeshare_.

Watch out: Seasonal restrictions on exchanging. Some resorts have rules that give owners preference for using their own timeshares during high season, and they prevent you from reserving and exchanging these high value weeks. If you want to exchange, you are forced to take a lower value week, which does not work in your favor. Fortunately, this is uncommon, and usually you can use your timeshare however you choose.

Special case - Save points by using a different system

If you own timeshare points, your company may be associated with one of the major exchange networks, and allow booking vacations using your points through their system. This can lead to some unexpected anomalies. Here is a recent real-life example.

▸ **Booking through your timeshare company**. You want to book at a particular resort in your own timeshare system. If you use your points to book a 2-bedroom there directly through your own club, it will cost 8400 points.

▸ **Booking through exchange company**. You can book the same exact resort and unit type through RCI, but it only requires 4800 points for you to do it that way.

▸ **Compare and save**. In this example, booking through RCI adds a $209 exchange fee to the transaction, but it saves you 3600 points. Knowing your cost per point (see *Tracking your cost of ownership*), you can determine whether booking through RCI is a better deal.

▸ **Points left for another trip**. After booking this vacation via the exchange company, you have 3600 points left over that you can apply to another vacation.

Expert tip: Compare costs through every avenue. It would be great if all timeshare companies gave their owners the best prices, but it's not always the case. Usually prices are more consistent than in this example, but oddities like this do exist. In this case, somebody was able to save 40% of their points by doing a little investigation into their options.

Special case - Book sooner through an exchange company

Here's another situation that can arise. There are times when you can book a sought-after reservation sooner by going through an exchange company than in your own system. If you wait to book it through your own company, your chances of getting a good reservation are slimmer because so many good weeks have already been snapped up.

Here's an example.

▸ **Booking window in your system**. Let's say you own points in a vacation club, and you want to book a trip to one of their resorts in Hawaii. The company rules specify

that the soonest you can book this using your points is 9
months in advance.

▸ **Booking window through exchange company**. Owners
at that specific resort can book their own week starting at
12 months out, and some of these weeks are deposited in
RCI. These would then be available for exchange in RCI,
as soon as they're deposited.

▸ **Book it sooner in RCI**. Putting in a Hawaii request early
in RCI may get you a reservation before your 9-month
booking window with your own points system even opens
up. With popular destinations and seasons, this can give
you an edge for getting what you want.

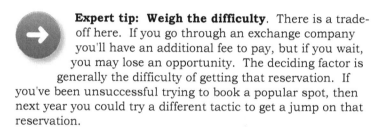

Expert tip: Weigh the difficulty. There is a trade-
off here. If you go through an exchange company
you'll have an additional fee to pay, but if you wait,
you may lose an opportunity. The deciding factor is
generally the difficulty of getting that reservation. If
you've been unsuccessful trying to book a popular spot, then
next year you could try a different tactic to get a jump on that
reservation.

Booking your week vs. taking the points

If you own a timeshare in a hybrid system, then you have a
choice between booking your week during a certain period, or
waiting and taking your points. For example, with Bluegreen,
you can reserve your week up to 13 months in advance.
Starting at 11 months out, you use points instead.

Sometimes your choice is obvious. Some people purposely buy
a week at a certain resort to get the advance reservation
priority there. Others buy strictly for points, with no thought
given to the underlying week at all.

Other times, you may need to weigh your options to make a
decision. Here are some considerations.

Do you own a high-demand week? If you own a specific week that's hard to get, this could be worth a premium to you in terms of exchange value, or on the rental market. You may find that you get more bang for your buck by reserving and exchanging your home week, or by renting out your home week and using the proceeds to rent elsewhere or purchase a getaway vacation.

Which fits your time frame best? Your points have an expiration date, and certain rules about how long you can extend them, and at what cost. If you want to book your own week, you have to use it, rent it, or deposit it before the date of that week. If you deposit it for exchange, you get additional time to use it, but you need to decide and deposit it well ahead of time, to maximize your trading power.

Can you get what you want with points? Some resorts and time periods are notoriously hard to get. In those places, the demand is high enough that many owners want to use their own weeks or rent them out, which means that those weeks aren't available to other points owners. In such a case, you might have a better chance of getting there by renting from another owner, and renting out your own timeshare to a third party to help cover costs.

What are you allowed to rent out? This depends on the rules for your timeshare. Are you allowed to rent out your home week? Are you allowed to rent out a timeshare stay that you book with points? Are you allowed to rent out points directly? If you're interested in pursuing renting as a way to recoup some of your annual fees, then find out the rules for your company so you know what your options are.

Exchanging back to your own resort

One trick that some timeshare owners employ is to use an exchange company to trade back to the same location where they own. Why? This can sometimes get you additional vacations and/or save you money. Here's how this strategy can work.

Exchange back for multiple weeks

The trading power system that is used in RCI gives you the ability to deposit a high value week, and get several lower value weeks in return, all from the same deposit.

Here's an example.

▸ **Start with a floating week**. Say you own a timeshare week with a 52-week float. Every week in the year is considered a red week, even though demand really varies considerably. This is not uncommon.

▸ **Maximize your deposit TPUs**. Use the RCI Deposit Calculator to find the most valuable week you can reserve. This gets you a deposit worth 23 TPUs. See *Maximizing your RCI trading power* for more tips.

▸ **Watch for low-TPU exchanges**. During low demand months, the resort is frequently not full, and there are often short-notice weeks available for as little as 5 TPUs.

▸ **Book multiple exchanges**. Using your 23 TPU deposit, you can book 4 separate weeks of vacation at your same resort, and have a 3 TPU deposit credit left over.

▸ **This can be a bargain**. The cost of your 4 vacation weeks is equal to your annual cost of ownership + the cost of the 4 exchanges. If the exchange fee is $209 per exchange, that means you're paying another $836 (4 times the fee) to get 4 weeks of vacation instead of 1. That puts the additional cost for the extra 3 weeks at $279/week (total $836 divided by 3 extra weeks). That's an excellent price for a week of vacation at a resort you enjoy.

Expert tip: Try this for off season and short notice. Many places, off season travel is wonderful, it's just less popular due to school schedules. When you can travel during the off season or shoulder season, and/or travel on short notice, you usually find better exchange values. This tactic lets you take advantage of those value discrepancies.

Exchange yours and book getaways

Another way you can take advantage of shoulder or off-season pricing or discounts for last minute travel, is to book inexpensive getaway, last call, or extra vacations to the destination where you own. Then you can deposit your own timeshare, maximizing it to get the highest trading power possible, and exchange it for travel elsewhere. Here's how it can work.

▸ **See if this looks possible**. Watch the Getaways on II, and the Extra Vacations and Last Calls on RCI. See what they have available for different seasons at your destination. If you see any resorts (not just your own), time periods, and prices that look attractive, this approach could work.

▸ **Deposit your timeshare for maximum value**. As with the last approach, you want to get maximum value for your own timeshare in the exchange system you're using. Book the highest demand week you can, and time your deposit so you get the most trade value possible.

▸ **Travel to your own location on getaways**. When you see good prices on getaways or extra vacations, use those to travel to the destination you own and love. You may even be able to get weeks there for less than $300 on last call. Meanwhile, you've got a high-value deposit with an exchange company that you can use for another vacation.

▸ **Check out other resorts**. This can be a great way to check out other resorts in your area. Sure, you love the resort where you own, but do you ever wonder what others are like? This approach may enable you to stay at a variety of resorts in the same area, and experience them first hand.

Expert tip: It's sad, but take advantage of it.
The sad fact of the matter is that in many locations,
owners of low or mid-season weeks pay more in
maintenance fees than renters pay for no-obligation
getaways. It's one of the downsides of timeshares, but
you might as well benefit from it. Buy those discount weeks
on extra vacations, and use your valuable timeshare
elsewhere.

**Expert tip: Comparison shop exchange
companies**. Many resorts are dual-affiliated with
both RCI and II, so you can find the same thing on
both systems. The same location can vary widely in
both availability and prices when you check both
websites. The smaller exchange companies also have weeks
for sale - their selection is more limited, but you may find a
good value.

Learn more: Shopping around for bargains.
Belonging to more than one exchange company may
cost more in terms of fees, but it can pay off when
you're getting a vacation. See *Comparison shopping
RCI and Interval International*, at
TimeshareGame.com/owners-guide-links/

Comparing exchange companies

The big two - RCI and II

Do you have a choice? Depending on what you own, you
may be tied to just RCI, just Interval International, or have the
option of using both. Many resorts now are dual-affiliated
though, which is ideal for owners because it gives you the
chance to choose yourself.

Quality of resorts. Between the big two, many people feel that
Interval International has a higher average quality of resorts.
It's true that II includes the Marriott and Starwood properties,

as well as many other upscale resorts. On the other hand, RCI includes the Hilton and Disney resorts, and has many other gold crown resorts as well. Though the average quality may be higher with Interval, you can certainly find excellent resorts in RCI as well.

Are you looking for specific properties? If you really want to stay at the Westin Ka'anapali on Maui, you will only find this on II. If you really want to stay at Disney's Animal Kingdom Villas, you will only find this on RCI. It may be difficult to get the trade you want, but if you want to have a chance, this could dictate which exchange company to use.

Number of resorts. RCI is the largest exchange company, with over 4,000 resorts worldwide. Interval International is second, with over 2,700 resorts. Though RCI has more locations to choose from, Interval has plenty of selection for most people's needs.

International coverage. Are you interested in traveling to exotic destinations? If so, this is where the selection of resorts could make a difference. If you want to travel to Switzerland, RCI has 15 resorts, while Interval has 6. It could be that you prefer some of the locations in Interval, but the added selection in RCI might make it easier to score a trade there.

Expert tip: Dual membership can make sense. If you have the option, joining both II and RCI can be beneficial. It does mean paying two membership fees, but having the ability to access and compare the offerings from both companies can more than make up for the additional fee. It all depends on how you use your membership.

The smaller exchange companies

The majority of timeshare owners make use of one or both of the major exchange companies. However, these two aren't the only game in town. There are a number of smaller exchange companies, and some people prefer using these to the big guys.

Lower fees. This is one of the biggest selling points for the smaller companies. Some of them have no membership fee. Most of them have lower exchange fees than the major companies. On the other hand, there's a trend toward offering "gold level" memberships for an annual fee, and some places charge upgrade fees too. While they may save you money, the cost savings on fees aren't always as large as you anticipate.

Personalized service. If you long for the days when you got to know people in a business and establish relationships, then this aspect of the smaller companies will appeal to you. Instead of dealing with a massive corporate call center, some owners get to know a representative who gives them personal assistance with arranging the trades they want.

Limited inventory. This is the biggest issue with using the small exchange companies. They don't get as many deposits, so there aren't as many timeshares for you to choose from. If you're searching for a hard-to-get destination, this will be more of an issue for you than if you're looking for an area with plenty of timeshares.

Specialized offerings. Some exchange companies have a specialty that makes them useful for certain people or in certain situations. Here are a couple of examples.

▸ **HTSE** - If you own in Hawaii, or want to exchange there, the Hawaii Timeshare Exchange could be useful for you.

▸ **SFX** - This company specializes in higher quality resorts, and won't accept everything. If you want to exchange your upper end timeshare, you may be able to find a high quality trade for it here.

You can find links and information for these and other exchange companies in the section *Timeshare exchange companies*.

Watch out: Geographic segregation may limit your selections. Dial an Exchange is the largest of the independent exchange companies, with worldwide operations. However, if you're looking for an international exchange, their system could pose a problem. Members in the US get access to US inventory. Members in Europe get access to European inventory. There's little cross-over, and if you're in the US looking for a European exchange, you could wait a long time without success.

Who has the best deals? You always want to get the best value for your timeshare when you deposit it. Sometimes a time-limited deal from one of the exchange companies could make the difference. If a company offers you 2-for-1 vacations during the month of February, that might be enough added value to tip the scales toward that option.

Expert tip: Don't put all your eggs in a small basket. When investigating the smaller exchange companies, start slow. If you own multiple timeshares, or a lock-off you can split, just deposit one to start with and see how it goes. Better yet, if the company lets you request first and deposit later, give that a try and see if they can come up with a match for what you want. You'd hate to have a lot of timeshare value tied up in a system that's not able to deliver what you want.

Comparing exchanges, getaways and rentals

Exchanging to other destinations is a great benefit of owning a timeshare, but it's not always the best way to go. You can often book the same vacation through other sources, too. If you've decided where and when you want to go, you can compare what's available through different avenues and what it costs, to determine your optimal choice.

Know your numbers. In comparing costs, the first thing you need to know is your cost of ownership. If you own points, what's your cost per point? If you own a week in II, what's your total annual cost? If you own a week with RCI, what's your total cost and your cost per TPU? There's more on these calculations in the section *How the Finances Work*.

Example - Comparing Orlando vacation options

Let's say you want to go to Orlando for a week in October, and stay at the Sheraton Vistana Resort. This resort is dual-affiliated with both RCI and Interval, so you could get here either way, depending on what you own. Running a few quick searches shows the following:

Possibilities through RCI:
- RCI points, 1BR, available for 37,500 points
- RCI weeks, 1BR, available on exchange for 20 TPUs
- RCI extra vacation, 1BR, available for $423

> ▸ For RCI points, what's your cost for 37,500 points? Take this and add the transaction fee of $159. Unless this is less than $423 (which would mean your points cost was less than $264, or $0.007/point), the extra vacation is a better deal.

> ▸ For RCI weeks, the exchange fee is $209, so unless the annual cost of 20 TPUs for you is less than $214 ($10.70/TPU), the extra vacation is a better deal.

Possibilities through II:
- II exchange, 1BR available on week-for-week exchange
- II getaway, no 1BR available, but 2BR is available for $427

> ▸ The exchange fee with II is $164, so unless the annual cost of your timeshare week is less than $263, the getaway is a better deal.

Possibilities through owner rentals:
- eBay.com has 1BR rentals available for $840 for the week
- Redweek.com owner rentals show no 1BR listed, but 2BR available at $800 for the week

> ▸ Owner rentals available are not close to matching the $423-427 for a week that RCI and II are offering.

Other sources:

- Sheraton.com, 1BR available at $165 per night ($1,155 for the week)
- Booking.com, 1BR available at $1,092 for the week

▸ The other websites are even more expensive than owner rentals.

Conclusion:

▸ For RCI, booking as an extra vacation is your best deal.

▸ For II, booking as a getaway is your best deal.

▸ If you have both II and RCI, you have a choice. Would you prefer a 1-bedroom for $423 (RCI) or a 2-bedroom for $427 (II)?

Additional considerations

Results can vary. In this example, booking a non-exchange vacation through RCI or II gives you the best price. However, in different cases your results can vary tremendously. Sometimes exchanging your week or using points is the best deal. Sometimes booking through a website like Booking.com gives you the best prices. Sometimes the only way to get what you want is to rent it from an owner.

Expert tip: Remember expiring points or deposits. If you have points or a deposited week that are going to expire soon, that can change the equation. Using your timeshare for an exchange vacation is better than letting it go to waste, even if you could have gotten a better deal via another channel. Whatever you do, make sure you get what value you can from those maintenance fees.

Traveling on short notice

Throughout this book, you have seen how planning far in advance can be useful for getting the best results with your timeshare. Of course, life doesn't always cooperate with planning a year or more in advance.

Sometimes work and family responsibilities mean that you can only plan trips close to your travel dates. Other times, you may just get the urge to go somewhere and want a quick getaway. When you want to take a trip SOON, without all the advance planning, here are some options.

Special deals with your timeshare. Check with your timeshare company or resort about any special deals they offer. Some companies have discount deals for short-notice vacations. Some resorts offer owners a "bonus time" stay, where you can pay for extra days at your timeshare. Check occasionally to see what's available.

Last Call Vacations (RCI). If your travel dates are 45 days or less in the future, then RCI Last Call vacations may have something for you. These are bargain vacations, with a fixed price based on unit size. Current prices range from $244 for a studio to $309 for a 2-bedroom. These are 7-night stays, but with those prices, it can be a good deal even if you only stay a few nights.

Inexpensive getaways (II and RCI). In Interval, Getaways are vacations you pay for directly, without exchanging. The same thing in RCI is called Extra Vacations. Whichever system you use, take a look at what they have. Often the prices go down for short notice trips. You don't have as much selection as you would booking early, but sometimes the prices are great.

Flexchange (II). Flexchange is II's term for exchanges done less than 60 days before check-in. This short-notice exchange inventory often includes units that become available due to late deposits or cancellations, and you can sometimes find amazing trades here, that you could never get normally. The inventory moves quickly, so search often, and if you see something good, be ready to jump on it right away. For more on this, see *Using Flexchange*.

Cheap exchanges (RCI). RCI doesn't have quite the same thing as Flexchange, but the concept of cheap last-minute exchanges works here, too. As the time gets closer to the check-in date, the TPUs required for an exchange typically drop. If you want an exchange in the next month or so, you can often see exchanges available for just 4 or 5 TPUs.

Watch for sales. RCI and other companies often send e-mail notifications when they're having a sale, and this can be a source of spontaneous vacation ideas. They could be advertising discount exchanges, bargains on extra vacations, or bonus weeks when you purchase a getaway. Sometimes this will be just the prompt you need to take an unplanned vacation.

Other uses of points

As mentioned in the section *Using points for airlines, cars and more*, owning points may give you a range of other ways to use them beyond booking a timeshare vacation. Often, points can be used to pay for hotel nights, airline tickets, car rentals or more.

There are a couple of approaches that are useful in figuring out whether you want to make use of these options.

Compare stand-alone costs. Check the cost of a specific item, such as a round trip plane ticket to Las Vegas, booked through different channels.

▸ You could book the ticket directly from the airline or through an online booking site, and pay with a credit card.

▸ You could use frequent flier miles or credit card rewards to pay for the ticket.

‣ You could use your timeshare points to pay for the ticket.

Once you know your timeshare cost per point (see *Costs of using/exchanging your points*), you can determine the real cost of using your timeshare points for the purchase. This lets you evaluate these options head to head, and see which gets you the best value.

Compare total vacation costs. You have options on how to pay for your resort stay - use your timeshare, buy a getaway or extra vacation, or rent from another owner. You also have options on how to pay for additional items like plane tickets and car rentals. The question is which gets you the best total package value, while also taking into consideration that your timeshare ownership needs to be paid whether you use it or not.

Here's an example:

‣ You're taking a trip to Lake Tahoe, and plan to book a timeshare stay with your points. You've checked on availability and alternatives, and have determined that using your points is definitely the way you want to go.

‣ You have significant points leftover from this, and don't anticipate having the time for another timeshare trip this year. What's the best thing to do with your leftover points? You could use them for other travel costs, or extend them to the next year. Here's how you could evaluate this.

Use points for -->	Airfare	Car rental	Extend to next year
How much you spend	- Cost of points - Car rental	- Cost of points - Airfare	- Cost of points - Airfare - Car rental - Fee to extend points
How much you save	- Cost savings on airfare	- Cost savings on car	- Nothing
What you have left	Nothing	Nothing	- Points for next year
Good if?	You get a good deal on airfare, compared to other methods.	You get a good deal on car rental, compared to other methods.	You think you'll get better use of your points next year, and don't mind paying the fee to extend.

Protecting your timeshare vacation

You have money invested in your timeshare, both from your initial payment price and your annual fees. You work on maximizing its value to get you the vacations you want. It would be a shame to see it all go to waste if some unexpected event meant that you couldn't take a planned vacation.

Depending on how you arrange your timeshare trip, you may have a few different options to protect your vacation.

Protection options for II vacations

E-Plus gives you low cost retrades. When you book an exchange on II, you give up your timeshare deposit for that trade. You can retrade it for something else later, for an additional exchange fee. If you cancel rather than retrade, you can get a replacement week, which also requires another exchange fee to use.

The optional E-Plus plan allows you to retrade up to 3 times. You pay $49 to add E-Plus to a specific exchange transaction, then pay no additional fees when you retrade it.

You can only purchase this within 5 days of confirming your original exchange, and must buy it before your vacation's check-in date. All retrades must occur within one year from the check-in date of your original exchange. E-Plus is not available for short stay exchanges or getaway vacations, and this option does not cover any other vacation-related costs.

Expert tip: Short notice retrades have limitations. If you do an E-Plus retrade less than 60 days before your check-in date, it is similar to using a flex deposit, in that you're limited to fairly short notice exchanges. Such a retrade can only be used for a new vacation starting 60 days or less after that check-in date.

Travel insurance offered by II. If you want to cover other aspects of your trip, II gives you an option to purchase travel insurance. This coverage, provided through Travel Guard, provides up to $1,000 for trip cancellation and interruption, $500 for loss of baggage and personal effects, and travel medical assistance. Complete details are available on the Interval website.

Protection options for RCI vacations

Trading Power Protection for RCI weeks. When you book an exchange vacation in RCI weeks, you use the trading power from a week you deposited. If you have to cancel your vacation, you get your deposit back, with a big caveat. The value of your deposit is recalculated based on your cancellation date, which means you could lose most (or all) of your deposit value.

An optional add-on of **Trading Power Protection** ensures that your full deposit trading power will be returned to your account in case of a cancellation. You can purchase this for $49 within 30 days of booking your exchange, or $89 after that.

Trading Power Protection does not cover your exchange fee, just the trading power you used. Once you receive the TPU's back in your account after a cancellation, you'll need to pay another exchange fee for a new transaction. This is not applicable to extra vacations or last call vacations.

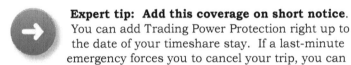

Expert tip: Add this coverage on short notice. You can add Trading Power Protection right up to the date of your timeshare stay. If a last-minute emergency forces you to cancel your trip, you can still buy this coverage. It won't cover other travel expenses, but at least you'll have your trading power back to use for another vacation.

Points Protection for RCI Points. When you cancel an RCI Points vacation, you get back some of your points, depending on when you cancel. If you cancel 120 days or more before your check-in date, you can get them all back. but after that you get fewer points returned as you get closer to the check-in date. If you cancel less than 30 days before your vacation date, you only receive 25% of your points back.

Optional **Points Protection** guarantees that you will get 100% of your points returned to your account in case of cancellation, no matter when you have to cancel. The cost is variable, depending on the vacation you have booked. You can only purchase this coverage (a) within 30 days of booking your points vacation, and (b) at least 14 days in advance of your check-in date.

Points Protection does not cover your transaction fee, just the points you used. When you decide to use those points again, you'll need to pay another transaction fee.

Other options for covering your vacation

Coverage via your timeshare company. If you book your timeshare vacation through your own timeshare company rather than going through RCI or II, check with them as to what protection options they offer.

Buying external travel insurance. If you want to purchase travel insurance, there are a number of companies that offer this. Many different plans are available, with different coverage details and costs. Typically plans cover trip cancellation or delay, lost or delayed baggage, emergency medical assistance, and more. A few companies to look at are Travel Insured, Travel Guard, and Travelex Travel Insurance, and there are others as well.

Note: As always, prices and terms are subject to change. The programs referred to in this section may be altered or discontinued at any time.

12. How the Finances Work

Fees, fees, fees...

Recurring fees

Usually paid annually, these are the fees you need to pay over and over. This is the on-going obligation you take on when you buy the timeshare. You have to pay these fees whether you use your timeshare or not.

* **Maintenance fees**. The cost of cleaning, managing, and maintaining the property is split between all of the owners, in the form of maintenance fees. Larger units, more deluxe resorts, and bigger points packages have higher maintenance fees.

Property taxes. Taxes depend on what you own and where you own it. The property taxes are often incorporated into your maintenance fees, but sometimes you'll see them broken out separately.

> **Expert tip: Itemized property taxes**. If property taxes are itemized on your bill, you may be able to count these on your tax return like other property taxes. Check with your accountant about your personal tax situation.

* **Club membership**. If your timeshare includes membership in a vacation club, there will be membership fees. These may be rolled into your maintenance fee or broken out separately.

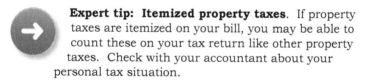

> **Watch out: Club fees can make a big impact**. Fixed club fees make it less attractive to own a small number of points. For example, if your base maintenance fee for a small package of points is $550, and the fixed club fee adds $319, that's a huge addition to your cost per point. Salespeople will point out that buying more points would lower your cost per point. Of

course, buying more points would also raise your overall payments, so don't buy more just to lower your costs.

✳ **Exchange membership**. If you want to exchange your timeshare through one of the major exchange companies, there is an annual membership fee. This covers you for a year, no matter how many exchanges you make during that time. In most cases this is optional, and if you don't anticipate trading then you don't need to pay it. Some timeshare companies automatically include a membership in your annual fees, in which case you don't have a choice in the matter.

Usage fees

These are fees that you only pay when you use your own timeshare, or exchange it and stay at a different property.

✳ **Reservation transaction fees**. When you use your points to book a stay at a resort there may be a transaction fee. The amount can vary depending on what company you're using, how long you stay, how you book the reservation, and how many reservations you have booked.

✳ **Account fees**. Depending on what timeshare companies you work with, you may have fees for managing your own timeshare account. Examples are fees to save, extend, pool, rescue, borrow or transfer your points. If you use RCI weeks, there is also a fee to combine your TPUs from multiple deposits.

✳ **Other fees**. Depending on what timeshare company you own with, you may have a range of other fees that could apply, such as upgrade fees or housekeeping fees.

✳ **Exchange fees**. When you use any of the exchange companies to trade your timeshare for a vacation at a different resort, you'll need to pay an exchange fee. This varies by company, but can be over $200.

✳ **Cancellation fees**. If you make a booking and then later cancel it, you will probably be out a cancellation fee or lose the exchange or transaction fee that you paid. This varies by company.

* **Guest certificates**. If you want to book a unit and let somebody else use it then you pay for a guest certificate. Some companies will give you a certain number of guest certificates for free, then you pay for any additional.

Resort fees

Individual resorts sometimes add on extra fees of their own. It's an unfortunate trend these days, with many airlines, hotels and timeshare resorts using add-on fees to increase their revenues. Often owners don't have to pay extra fees to stay at their own timeshare, but if you want to stay somewhere else, then watch for added fees like these.

* **Resort fees**. Just like hotels, some timeshare resorts now charge a daily "resort fee," that covers the use of the pool, exercise room and other facilities. Sometimes this covers internet access, other times that is a separate charge. Usually this is mandatory, even if you never use any of those facilities.

* **Parking fees**. At some resorts, you might need to pay up to $30/day extra for parking.

* **Registration fees**. Some resorts charge a flat registration fee to everyone when they arrive to check in to the resort.

* **Housekeeping fees**. You'd think that housekeeping would be included in the cost of staying at a resort. Usually it is, but some resorts charge an additional "housekeeping fee." This is fairly common for RCI points.

* **Occupancy tax**. Some locations have an occupancy tax they will add onto your bill.

 Watch out: All inclusive fees. Some resorts have a mandatory all-inclusive fee, that covers all your food and drinks while you're there. It's a nice concept, but the fees can be huge, about $1000 per person for a week's stay.

 Learn more: All about all inclusive fees. Find out what to watch for when it comes to all-inclusive vacations, along with an analysis of whether and when they could make sense for you. See _All-inclusive fees can multiply your costs_, at _TimeshareGame.com/owners-guide-links/_

Special assessments

Special assessments only happen occasionally (thank goodness). These are not normal or recurring expenses. They are special costs to pay for major repairs or upgrades, which are over and above your regular maintenance fees. For more on how these work, see the section _Special Assessments_.

Tracking your cost of ownership

Owning a timeshare means that you incur certain expenses year after year, whether you use it or not. This is your basic cost of ownership, and it will change from year to year, generally in an upward direction. Tracking these numbers helps you...

* Understand the financial impact of your timeshare ownership

* See how your timeshare costs change over time

* Plan the cost of future timeshare vacations

* Decide if and when it's time to get rid of a timeshare

Timeshare weeks

Key numbers for timeshare weeks:

▸ Total timeshare cost per year

▸ Cost per TPU (if you use RCI weeks for exchanges)

Ownership costs (week)	2014	2015	2016
Annual maintenance fee	775	830	
Property taxes	42	44	
Other timeshare fees	---	---	
Total timeshare cost per year	817	874	
TPUs received (RCI weeks) *	27	28	
Your cost per TPU*	$30.26	$31.21	

TPUs are a measure of trading power used in RCI weeks. If you're not using RCI weeks, ignore these figures.

The **cost per TPU** is the number you need for planning the cost of exchange vacations with RCI. The table above shows a sample calculation.

Timeshare points

Key numbers for timeshare points:

▸ Total timeshare cost per year

▸ Your cost per point

Ownership costs (points)	2014	2015	2016
Number of points	60,500	60,500	60,500
Annual maintenance fee	848	912	

Ownership costs (points)	2014	2015	2016
Annual membership fee*	124	124	
Other annual timeshare fees	---	---	
Total timeshare cost per year	972	1,036	
Your cost per point	$0.016	$0.017	

Annual membership fee is included here only if it is a mandatory fee, and not already rolled into the maintenance fees.

The **cost per point** is the number you need to plan the cost of future vacations, and to compare the cost of different ways to use your timeshare points.

Costs of using/exchanging your week

When you own a week, using your own timeshare is often the most economical way to vacation. On the other hand, one of the big benefits of owning a timeshare is the ability to exchange it for vacations around the world. Knowing the costs involved lets you evaluate your options on a financial basis, and make informed decisions about your vacation plans.

Using your own week. Normally the cost for using your own timeshare week is just the cost of ownership. Most add-on costs like resort fees don't apply to owners at a timeshare, only to exchangers. There are exceptions, though, like timeshares that charge a daily parking fee even for owners.

Week for week exchanges. If you use a week-for-week exchange, then it's fairly simple to calculate the cost of the exchange week you get based on the cost of the week you own plus fees.

TPU based exchanges. If you use RCI weeks, then your exchanges are based on TPUs (trading power units). You could get multiple exchanges from a single deposit, or use multiple deposits to book a single exchange. The costs of your exchange vacation are based on your cost per TPU, rather than the overall cost of the week you own.

Key numbers for using / exchanging a week:

▸ Total cost per week of timeshare vacation

▸ Cost per night

Costs for timeshare week	Use week	II	RCI
Total cost of your timeshare week	874	874	874
Your cost per TPU (RCI)	---	---	$31.21
Exchange company membership	---	89	89
Exchange fee paid	---	174	209
Other exchange company fees*	---	0	0
Resort fees	0	50	50
# of TPUs used for exchange	---	---	25
Cost of TPUs used for exchange	---	---	780
Total cost for the week	874	1,187	1,128
Timeshare cost per night	125	170	161

* *Other fees such as an extend deposit fee or combine deposit fee.*

The **cost per night** is useful for comparing your timeshare vacation to other types of holidays. For example, what would it cost to stay at a comparable hotel in that location?

Allocating membership cost for multiple vacations. The table above includes the entire cost of the exchange company membership in the calculation. If you book more than one vacation through the same company (whether an exchange or a purchased vacation), then you need to split the cost of the membership between that many vacations. For instance, if you take two II vacations in a year, then you'd allocate $44.50 for the membership fee to each trip ($89 divided by 2).

Expert tip: Calculating blended TPU costs. If you own multiple timeshares that you use in RCI weeks, then you could be using TPUs for an exchange that come from different deposits. For instance, you could deposit a week in Orlando and a week in Sedona, and use a combined deposit to get a week in Hawaii. This table gives an example of the blended TPU calculations.

Blended TPU cost	
Annual cost, Sedona week	874
Annual cost, Orlando week	569
Combine deposit fee	109
Total cost of combined deposits	1,552
TPUs for Sedona deposit	29
TPUs for Orlando deposit	15
Total TPUs received	44
Blended cost per TPU	$35.27

Expert tip: Splitting the costs for a lock-off. If you own a lock-off timeshare week that you split into separate deposits, then your maintenance fee covers more than one exchange week. In RCI, this is covered with the TPU calculations, but if you use your week or exchange it elsewhere, you can allocate the costs yourself. Estimate your own percentages for how much value each side of your lock-off is worth, with the larger section getting the higher value.

Split lock-off costs	
Annual cost, 2-bedroom lock-off	874
Percentage to 1-bedroom side	60%
Percentage to studio side	40%
Allocated cost for 1-bedroom	524
Allocated cost for studio	350

Costs of using/exchanging your points

When you own timeshare points, you can use your cost per point to estimate and compare the cost of different points vacations. The following table shows a couple of examples featuring different vacation options.

Key numbers for using / exchanging points:

▸ Total cost per timeshare vacation (may not always be a full week)

▸ Cost per night

Costs for points vacations	Cape Cod week	California getaway
Your cost per point	$0.017	$0.017
Destination / resort	Cape Cod	California
What you're booking	2-bedroom	1-bedroom
Season booked	High (summer)	Mid (fall)
Number of nights	7	4
# of points required	54,500	38,400
Cost for the required points	927	653
Reservation transaction fee	159	99
Fees to borrow/save points, etc.	---	---
Other timeshare/resort fees	49	100
Total cost for timeshare stay	1,135	852
Timeshare cost per night	162	213

The key input to these calculations is your cost per point, calculated earlier. A key output is the **cost per night**. You can compare that to what it would cost you for alternate accommodations in the same area.

Exchange costs with points. If you use your timeshare points through an exchange company, the cost calculations are almost the same. Just be sure to add any additional exchange company costs.

Costs of other timeshare trips

Extra vacations and Getaways. When you purchase an Extra Vacation or Last Call vacation from RCI, or a Getaway from Interval International, you don't need to exchange your timeshare, you just pay for the vacation. Calculating the cost of these vacations is straightforward.

Costs for extra vacation	
Vacation price, including tax	495
Exchange company membership*	30
Other exchange company fees	0
Resort fees	49
Total cost for timeshare stay	574
Timeshare cost per night	82

* Membership fee, allocated over annual number of vacations with that company.

Bonus exchange weeks. If you use Interval International, you may get extra vacation weeks through an Accommodation Certificate or with an XYZ. (For more about these, see *Getting extra weeks with II*.) If you go through one of the smaller exchange companies, you may get a bonus week as a deposit incentive. However you come by them, it's fairly simple to calculate the cost of these vacations. They usually turn out to be a great deal!

Costs for bonus week	
Exchange company membership*	30
Exchange / reservation fee	174

Costs for bonus week	
Other exchange company fees	0
Resort fees	55
Total cost for timeshare stay	259
Timeshare cost per night	37

* *Membership fee, allocated over annual number of vacations with that company.*

Using points for other items. One oft-cited benefit of timeshare points is that you can use your points to pay for plane tickets, hotel stays, or other vacation expenses. It's smart to work out the actual cost of doing it this way, and compare it to the cost of booking through other channels.

Costs for other points uses	
Your cost per point	$0.017
# of points required	31,000
Cost for the required points	527
Booking transaction fee	52
Other fees	0
Total cost using your points	579

Now that you know the cost of booking this deal with your points, you can compare this with how much it would cost through another channel. You may find that this is a good deal, but often it is not the most economical way to go.

Total vacation costs

So far, this section has focused on just timeshare-related costs, but the overall cost of a vacation includes more than just the price of accommodations. You also need to cover the costs of transportation, food, recreational activities, and more. Of course, you need to figure in all of those costs when you're budgeting for a vacation, whether it's a timeshare trip or not.

When you're looking at timeshare options, it's a good idea to at least have these in mind, even if you don't fill out a spreadsheet for them. That timeshare deal in St. Kitts may be a bargain, but once you add in airfare for your family, the financial implications can be very different.

13. Creating Your Timeshare Calendar

As discussed in earlier sections, planning ahead gives you the best chance to maximize the value you get from your timeshare. Reservations, deposits, and exchange requests may need to be done many months in advance to get you the optimal results.

With timeframes a year or more in the future, it's easy to lose track of what needs to happen when. What do you need to do this month, to get things lined up for your timeshare vacation next summer? If you don't stay on top of things, you may miss out. Here's what can happen.

* **You can't get the reservation** you want, because those dates were snapped up as soon as they opened for reservations.

* **You lose trading power** for your exchange because you waited too long to deposit your timeshare.

* **You miss the exchange** you want because you didn't have a search going in time to catch a bulk deposit.

This is where **creating your own timeshare calendar** becomes important. You can plan out what needs to happen when, working backward from key dates like vacations you want to book. Once you have everything in your calendar, a reminder system helps you take care of timeshare tasks at the optimal time, so you get the most out of your ownership.

Your timeshare calendar **isn't a static document** that you set up and hang on the wall. Instead, it will continue to evolve over time. Each year brings new opportunities, new tasks, and new vacations. You'll continue to find new places to go, and techniques you want to try. As you achieve more success, you may decide to expand your timeshare portfolio, increasing the complexity of your scheduled tasks.

Through all of this, your timeshare calendar is a way to keep things organized. **It's a working system**, that assists you in making the best use of your ownership. This section will walk you through things to consider as you create your personal timeshare calendar.

Planning styles

With timeshares, it is often necessary to do things well in advance to get the best results. However, people are different in how far ahead they like to plan, how far in advance they can plan (due to work schedules etc.), and how structured they like to be.

Because of these variations, this book breaks planning advice into three broad categories.

- **Planner**. If you're a highly organized person who enjoys planning vacations, and are able to make at least some of your arrangements far in advance, then this is for you. This route will involve the most advance planning.

- **Opportunist**. If you're not much of a planner, and prefer to operate in a relatively off the cuff manner, grabbing opportunities when they arise or when the mood strikes, this is for you. This path requires the least advance planning.

- **Combination**. Many people will fall into this category, which is a bit of both. For instance, you may arrange big vacations far in advance (following the Planner's timeline), but keep your options open for shorter, less expensive trips (like the Opportunist).

In the following sections, you'll see suggested steps to follow depending on your planning style.

If you're an opportunist, the thought of all this advance planning may have you running for the hills. Don't worry - you don't need to do it all. You can pick your path based on your personal preferences.

Your vacation wish list

Where do you want to go? When do you want to go? Your
wish list is the foundation for your timeshare planning. Once
you know what you're aiming for, then you can figure out how
to get it.

Planning styles and your wish list

Planner	Opportunist	Combination
Keep a list looking at least 2 years into the future, possibly much more.	Keep ideas in your head, but no official list. Stay open to new thoughts and opportunities.	Plan major vacations more than a year in advance. Smaller trips can be off the cuff.
You'll want to do all of these steps.	You'll make many of these same decisions, but not in this step-by-step process.	You can do a short version of these steps.

Wish list, step by step

Where do you want to go? Do you want to lie in a hammock
under a palm tree? Swoosh down the slopes in the Alps?
Watch the kids shriek with delight at Disney World? All of the
above? Whatever you want, put it on your list. At this point,
your ideas could be very specific (your home resort),
moderately specific (Austria in the winter), or just a rough idea
(a tropical beach resort).

Browse your member guide for ideas. If you own timeshare
points, then your member guide describes where you can go

and how many points it takes for different resorts. This can be a good source of vacation ideas.

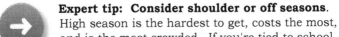

Expert tip: Use RCI's vacation type search for ideas. Say you're looking for a beach vacation, but you're not tied to a specific destination. In RCI, searching by "Vacation type = Beach" can show you many places you might not have considered. What about Costa Rica, or the Costa del Sol in Spain? This is a great way to find new ideas.

Who's going with you? Do you envision this spot for a family vacation? A romantic getaway? A large family reunion? The size of your group will determine the accommodations you need. It can also affect your scheduling - like limiting family trips to school vacation times.

How long do you want to stay? Is this somewhere you'd want to stay for a week? A quick trip that's just a few days? A longer trip, like an overseas trip where you want to make the most of the airfare and travel time?

What time of year do you want? What's the weather like at that destination? Are you looking for a specific season? What work or school schedules do you need to plan around? Make this as broad as you can while still getting what you want. It's easier to get "July or August" than it is to get "August 12-19."

Expert tip: Consider shoulder or off seasons. High season is the hardest to get, costs the most, and is the most crowded. If you're tied to school vacation schedules, this may be what you need. However, shoulder season can have fine weather too, and even off-season travel has its benefits. One of my favorite trips to Italy was in January. It was chilly, but it felt more authentic when we weren't surrounded by throngs of tourists.

Start assigning trips to years. Where do you want to go this year, next year, and the year after? Start slotting the vacations you want into years. Having at least 2 years of trips identified will help you get plans in place far enough ahead. You can set tentative plans even further out, if you want.

How do your own timeshares fit? If you own a week, are some of your vacations stays at your own resort? If you own points, which of the places on your wish list are in your points system? For a vacation where you can't use your own timeshare, is an exchange a possibility?

Look at destinations and resorts. Let's say you're thinking of the Greek Islands. Start looking at what's available. Which islands look the best, what resorts are in the area, and which of them seem appealing? Would you want to combine multiple locations into one extended vacation?

Start watching your future destinations. If you're planning to use your own timeshare week or points, how far in advance do bookings tend to fill up? For exchanges, what do you see on occasional manual searches? How about extra vacations or getaways - what do you see available, and at what prices?

Expert tip: Keep notes on destinations. Keep notes of all the information you pick up in your research. For example, does your own timeshare company have the resort you want? Is it tough to get into during prime season? Does II or RCI have better exchanges in a location? Did you find 5 resorts there that you'd love to get? Any information like this can be useful in making plans.

Adjust timing based on what you find. Let's say that you want to go to Tuscany, and you were thinking about June. You might find that this is a difficult month to get, but that if you can do April or early May there are better options, both as far as timeshare availability and airfare.

Planning your weeks use

If you own a timeshare week, this section is for you. If you own points and not weeks, skip ahead to _Planning your points use_.

Planning styles and using your week

Planner	Opportunist	Combination
You'll want to follow all of these steps.	To get high-demand weeks, you will need these advance planning steps.	Follow all of these steps.
Book as far ahead as the rules allow to ensure you get the best time periods.	For locations and seasons with plenty of space, spur of the moment is fine.	Plan as far ahead as needed for high season or max trade / rent value.

* Many of these steps are related to floating weeks. If you own a fixed week, you can skip everything related to getting certain dates.

Planning your week, step by step

Decide how to use your week. Will you be using your own timeshare, or exchanging it? Do you want to rent it out to somebody else? If you have a lock-off, would you keep the full unit together, or split it?

Decide on the dates you want. Depending on how you will use your week, select your dates and make a note of them.

● **Personal use** - Just select the dates you want to use your timeshare.

● **Exchange** - If you're going to deposit your week with an exchange company, can you pick the week yourself? If so,

then what week will give you the greatest trading value?
(See *Maximizing your RCI trading power* or *Maximizing your II trading power*.

- **Renting it out** - If you're planning to rent your week out, what week will have the highest rental demand?

Determine the lead time you need. What are the rules for booking lead time at your timeshare? If you want a popular week, you may need to move fast. At some resorts, peak weeks or holidays can fill up within minutes. If you can book 13 months in advance, then you might need to book exactly that day, first thing in the morning.

Not all resorts or seasons demand such quick action, and for low season, you can often wait until shortly before your trip. You can learn from experience and other owners what the situation is where you own.

Note dates for your planning calendar. For each timeshare week, you'll have at least two dates for your planning calendar, possibly more.

☑ **Vacation start date**. The check-in date that you want to reserve.

☑ **Booking date**. The date to make your reservation.

☑ **Deposit date**. The date to deposit it with an exchange company.

Make your reservations. You know when you want your vacation to start, and you know how much booking lead time you need. Schedule a reminder to make your reservation on the appropriate day.

Expert tip: Biennial and triennial timelines. If you own a biennial or triennial timeshare, it can be even more important to note these dates on your calendar. With an annual, you may do the same thing every year so it's relatively fresh in your mind. With a triennial, it is three years between each usage, and the last thing you want to do is forget about it and miss an opportunity.

Expert tip: Standardize process for repeated vacations. If you book the same vacation in multiple years, you can get this down to a routine. For example, some people who know they always want a prime week that's hard to get, simply plan to call every year at 8am exactly 12 months before. Doing this every year makes it a simple, easy routine.

Planning your points use

If you own timeshare points, this section is for you. If you own a timeshare week and not points, use the section *Planning your weeks use*.

Planning styles and using your points

Planner	Opportunist	Combination
Follow all of these steps.	You'll need to do these steps, but informally is fine unless you want peak season or holidays.	Follow all of these steps.
Book as far ahead as you can, and track all your points and activities carefully.	Spur of the moment is fine for non-peak trips, but stay on top of deadlines and expiration dates.	Plan as far ahead as needed for what you want. Track expiration dates and action deadlines.

Planning your points, step by step

Decide how to use your points. Which places on your wish list can you book with your points? Which places can you get by exchanging? If you can't use your points for a vacation, can you rent them out and pocket the cash? The goal is to figure out what to do with your points each year, so that you either make good use of them, or take action so they don't expire.

Decide what to book. Determine where and when you want to book trips using your points.

● **Personal use** - Decide the resort and dates you want, and verify the points required for your reservation.

● **Renting it out** - If you're planning to book a vacation and then rent it out, what resort and dates will give you the greatest payback in terms of rental income? Verify how many points this will require.

Determine the lead time you need. When do reservations open for the spots you want? How far in advance do you need to book? Some places and seasons will be difficult to get and require early action, while others will be far easier.

Do you need to save or extend points? If you may not use all of your timeshare points in a year, then think about saving or extending them. If you want to do that, what's the deadline to take action? Double check your dates so that you don't miss your chance to get an extension.

Watch out: Plan ahead for extending your points. Some timeshare companies limit your ability to save or extend your points once you are partway through the year. In some cases, even the first day of the year is too late! If your timeshare works like this, you need to make decisions far in advance. If there's a chance you may have extra points one year, note the cut-off dates on your calendar, so you can take action early to extend them.

Do you need to borrow or rent more points? What if the vacations you want to book require more points than you have? Can you borrow the extra points from a future year? Can you rent them from the company, or from a third party? Rules vary by company, so determine what your best option is.

Note dates for your planning calendar. You'll have a number of dates for your planning calendar, depending on what you want to do:

☑ **Points received date**. What date will your next allocation of points be placed in your account?

☑ **Deadline to save/extend points**. If you want to save or extend your points for future use, what's the deadline date to do that?

☑ **Vacation dates**. What are your desired check-in and check-out dates?

☑ **Booking date**. For a vacation you want, what's your target date to make the reservation?

☑ **Points expiration date**. Each set of points in your account will have an expiration date. Make sure you do something with them before this time.

Reserve high-demand vacations. These are the vacations you need to plan fairly far in advance. The greater the demand for the resort and date range you want, the more important it is to make your reservations at the right time.

Book short notice getaways. If you haven't used all of your points yet, you'll have some available for short notice getaways. You don't need to do a lot of planning for these. Just check what's available now and then and book something that looks like fun.

Planning your exchanges

Two approaches to planning exchanges

If you want to exchange your timeshare to go somewhere else, there are two fundamentally different ways to go about this.

- **Maximize deposit, then wait and see**. This is good if you have a timeshare you know you're not going to use yourself, but you haven't decided where you want to go. You deposit your timeshare with an exchange company to lock in your maximum trading power. You then have a couple of years or so to decide how to use it.

- **Plan the exchange, start to finish.** This approach is if you have a specific vacation you want. You select your desired destination first, then determine how you can use a timeshare exchange to get there, and make your plans accordingly. Your vacation goal drives all the planning.

The first is easiest, so let's start there.

Maximize the deposit, then wait and see

Planner	Opportunist	Combination
Deposit your timeshare before it starts to lose trading power.	Deposit your timeshare before it starts to lose trading power.	Deposit your timeshare before it starts to lose trading power.

Choose your exchange company. You may be locked into one of the major exchange companies, but if you have a choice, which of them tends to get you the best exchanges? You can also consider one of the smaller companies.

Maximize your deposit trading power. You always want to get the most trade value possible. Check the tips in _Maximizing your RCI trading power_ or _Maximizing your II_ _trading power_. If you're using an independent exchange company, see what deposit specials they offer.

Note dates for your planning calendar:

☑ **Date to deposit timeshare**. When should you make the deposit, to get the maximum exchange value?

☑ **Deposit expiration date**. You typically have a couple of years from your deposit's check-in date to find an exchange and take your vacation. Note the expiration date, so that you don't wait too long and let it expire.

Plan the exchange, start to finish

This route is considerably more complicated, but it can enable you to get a timeshare vacation that you really want. If you're longing for a hard-to-get vacation, then this approach will give you the best chance of getting it. Planners will love this, but opportunists, not so much!

Planner	Opportunist	Combination
Follow all these steps.	Just do the basics to set up deposits and search for exchanges.	Do a short version of these steps.
You can start research steps years in advance, and begin search requests up to 2 years beforehand.	Start searches whenever you think of it, and deposit timeshare when needed.	Start search requests for big or difficult vacations 1+ years in advance, use shorter time for others.

Research locations and resorts. This builds on the notes you took on your wish list. As your desired vacation gets closer, you move from general looking around, to focused research.

Make a list of the resorts you want. Do manual searches now and then to see what's available, and where the most inventory is. Remember that manual searches only show the "leftovers" after on-going searches are filled, so you may not see a lot.

Choose an exchange company. Which company looks like the best bet for getting the vacation you want? You don't need to set this in stone until it's time to deposit your timeshare, but you can narrow it down at this point.

Start looking at trading power or points required. Check points charts to see how many points you'd have to spend for different resorts and seasons. If you're exchanging a week, manual searches can give you a feel for the trading power you'll need. This can be tough in II - if you don't see anything, you don't know if it's because there's nothing available, or because your week doesn't have enough trading power.

Weeks - Figure out your deposits. What will you use as your trade for this exchange?

▸ Do you need to deposit a week, or do you already have a deposited week on hand with a travel window that fits the trip you want?

▸ What deposit (or combination of deposits in RCI) would you need in order to have enough trading power?

Points - Figure out your points. Determine how many points you need, and the best way to get them.

▸ Do you have enough points to book what you want?

▸ Do you need to save or extend points from an earlier year?

▸ Do you need to borrow or rent points to add some more?

Determine the lead time you need. This is based on a couple of things.

▸ Difficulty of exchange. The more difficult an exchange is to book (higher demand and lower availability), the more lead time you want to allow with your request.

▸ Lead time allowed. How soon can you start a search? How far in advance can you reserve and deposit your week or points? Can you start a search before you make a deposit?

Expert tip: Lead time is vacation specific. If your goal is to take the kids to Orlando, you don't need a lot of lead time, because there is almost always something available in Orlando. On the other hand, if you want to stay at Disney's Animal Kingdom, you'd better get your request in earlier, because that resort has high demand and limited supply.

Decide when to start your search. If you're looking for a tough trade, start your request as early as possible. Working more than a year in advance can help with this. If you're looking for a place that has adequate supply, or you're not looking for peak season, you can start much closer to your vacation time.

Deposit first or request first? Depending on what exchange company you're using, you may not have any choice on this. However, if you have a chance to choose, this is a fundamental decision to make. For more, see _Deposit first vs. Request first in II_.

Decide when to deposit your timeshare. With a deposit-first search, you need to get your timeshare deposited before you can start the search. If you're using a request-first search, you don't have this constraint. It's still wise to set a deadline for making your deposit though, so you don't lose too much trading power while waiting for a search to produce results.

Expert tip: Use multiple request first searches. Using a request-first search means you don't commit your timeshare to an exchange company until they find you a match. This means you could set up a request-first search with more than one company, and have them all working your search concurrently. As soon as you get a match from one place, confirm that exchange, then cancel your other searches.

Expert tip: Plan an extended vacation with multiple searches. If you're planning a longer vacation, you may have more than one search running at a time. Say you want to do a 2-week Hawaii trip in February or March that visits Maui and the big island. You could have one search running for each island, both of which are for the entire 2-month window you want. When either search matches, adjust the dates on the other search to look for the week before or after the reservation you have confirmed.

What's your fallback plan? Let's say you want a spring break trip to Aruba. You've had a request running for months, but it hasn't turned up anything yet. At what point to do you make other plans? Do you have another destination, a less desirable resort, or a different time period you might want? Decide on a "plan B date." If you haven't gotten the exchange you want by that date, you can cancel the search and go with plan B instead.

Expert tip: Book a hotel as a fallback plan. If you really want to do Aruba for spring break, you could book a hotel there that lets you cancel with no penalty. This way, you can go ahead and book your airfare without worrying about whether you can make the trip. If your timeshare search works, that's great - just cancel the hotel. If your exchange doesn't work out, then stay at the hotel. This tactic lets you keep a search running until the last minute, while avoiding expensive last-minute airfare.

Note dates for your planning calendar. You'll have a number of dates for your planning calendar:

☑️ **Date to start search**. When do you want to start the search request(s) for your vacation?

☑️ **Date to deposit timeshare**. When do you want to deposit your timeshare with the exchange company? For a request-first search, this date will be determined by when you get a match on your request, but it's wise to have a "drop dead deposit date" anyway. When that date comes, deposit your timeshare, match or no match, to avoid losing your trading power.

☑️ **Plan B date**. When would you pull the plug on an unsuccessful search, and go with plan B for your vacation instead?

Planning your finances

Normal timeshare expenses are pretty predictable. You have maintenance fees that you pay every year or every month. There are a few situations that will require a little planning, though.

Advance reservations that require advance fees. This is quite common. If you want to book a reservation as far in advance as possible to get the best dates locked in, you may need to pay the maintenance fees for that period in advance.

For example, say you want to book a March 2016 reservation one year in advance to get the dates you want. If you need to pay the fees before you can book it, you'd need to pay your 2016 fees by March 2015. If the normal due date for those fees was January 1, that would mean paying about 10 months before the normal due date, and it could mean paying 2015 and 2016 fees just a couple of months apart.

Expert tip: Stay ahead of the curve on fees. If you're in this situation, get ahead of the curve and stay there. If you pay each year's fees in advance, then you'll get into a pattern where you're still paying one year worth of fees every year - it will just be the year ahead. That will ensure you're always paid up in time to get the best reservations.

Double vacation costs one year. If you're saving or extending your points, or depositing a week for a future exchange, it's kind of like a layaway plan. You pay the fees now, but you get the value in a future year. The only issue is that if you're taking a non-timeshare vacation this year, it means double vacation costs this year (the cost of your non-timeshare vacation + your normal timeshare fees for the year).

Tying up your money on rentals. If you're getting into renting timeshares, you will need to plan for the cash flow lag time. You need to pay your timeshare fees in order to make the reservations you want, and then it could be quite a few months before you get payment back for that reservation from a renter. The more rentals you do, the more funds you can have tied up this way.

Note dates for payments. For planning purposes, note the dates when you need to make timeshare payments on your calendar. If you've determined that you want to make a reservation on June 11, and you know that you need to have your fees paid before you can do that, then add a reminder to pay your fees a few days before that, so everything is ready to go.

Your personal timeshare calendar

Keeping track of what needs to be done when, is a key to getting the maximum value from your timeshare. Booking reservations, making deposits, and setting up searches at the optimum time can greatly improve your results. A good tool for staying on top of it all is your personal timeshare calendar. Here are some ideas.

Choose your platform

It makes sense to use a tool that you're comfortable with, and one that fits with how you track other activities. You can keep your timeshare plans in the same place you track everything from the kids' vacations to dental appointments. Just go with something that's easy for you to use.

● **Paper vs. Computer calendars**. Some people like paper calendars, while others prefer a computerized system like Outlook or Google Calendar. Paper calendars are very visual, and have the advantage of simplicity. You can also add post-it notes, or paper clip items right to your calendar. Computer-based calendars make it easier to reschedule items, and can also send you reminders when it's time to do something. It's just a personal preference which you choose.

● **Calendar vs. Planning spreadsheet**. You may want to use a spreadsheet rather than a real calendar. A spreadsheet makes it easier to calculate dates (e.g. 45 days before August 22). On the other hand, a calendar will show both your timeshare and non-timeshare activities, which can be important when you're planning vacations.

● **Combination**. Sometimes a combination approach works well. For instance, you could track tentative vacation plans in Excel, and transfer them to your paper calendar once they're confirmed.

What to include on your calendar

☑ **Vacation dates, tentative and solid**. When you have decided on a vacation you want to take (even if it's not arranged yet), enter the dates on your calendar, so you can easily see what you've got in the works.

☑ **Dates to make reservations**. When you know what you want to book, note your target date to make that reservation on your calendar, so that you don't miss your chance to book a high-demand vacation.

☑ **Dates to make deposits**. You get more value from depositing your timeshare with an exchange company far enough in advance. Keeping this on your calendar helps make sure you get maximum trade value.

☑ **Deadline dates.** You may have deadline dates if you want to save or extend your points. You could have a date to use your week, before it turns to points. Note any important deadline dates on your calendar.

☑ **"Plan B" dates**. If you are waiting for a timeshare exchange, it is wise to have a "plan B," in case you don't get the exchange you want. Decide when you need to take action for "plan B," and note those dates.

☑ **Dates to pay fees**. Note when you need to pay timeshare fees. You may also want to note the expected amount here, to make it easier to see if you need to rearrange funds beforehand.

☑ **Rental dates**. If you're renting out your timeshare, you may have tasks for advertising, getting guest certificates, etc. Decide when these need to be done and add them to your calendar. You can also note rental details like the renter's name and check-in date.

Building a working system

Your timeshare calendar is not just a static document that you print and stick in a binder. To be effective, you need a working system that continues to evolve and change as you create and finalize plans, and one that provides timely reminders that help you make the most of your timeshare.

Here's a process that will turn your calendar into a working system.

Enter tentative plans. As you come up with new vacation plans, enter the target dates in your system. If you decide you want to visit Myrtle Beach next August, put that on your calendar. Planning back from there, enter the associated task dates. When do you need to book the reservation? If it's an exchange, when are you going to start a search request?

Get your reminders in place. If you've determined that the best time to deposit your week is next March, then set up a tickler to remind you to do this when the time comes. This could be an automated reminder or just a yellow sticky note on your computer. Whatever your system, make sure you have a way of reminding you when these important "to do" dates arrive.

Track confirmed vacations. Once a vacation is confirmed, change it from tentative to definite. This might mean changing pencil to pen on a paper calendar, or updating a status on a spreadsheet. Then figure out what else this will affect. Is there something else you'd like to plan before or after this? If it's an II exchange, does this open up an XYZ opportunity?

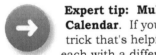
Expert tip: Multiple calendars in Google Calendar. If you use this tool for planning, one trick that's helpful is to set up multiple calendars, each with a different color. For example, you could have yellow for tentative plans, blue for confirmed vacations, and red for tasks to do and deadline dates. When a vacation changes from tentative to confirmed status, just change which calendar it's on and add any new details, like confirmation number or check-in time.

Add secondary tasks. After you've booked your timeshare stay, there are usually related tasks to do. This could include booking plane tickets, a hotel night before or after, or a rental car. You may want to put these items on your calendar, start a separate checklist for each trip, or keep a planning folder for each trip where you collect itineraries and confirmations.

Do a monthly review. Once a month or so, review your timeshare plans. Take a look at your calendar and your tracking spreadsheets. Do you have any deadline dates approaching? An unproductive search you may want to modify? Is there a blank space on the calendar you'd love to fill with a trip? A monthly review is a great way to keep your timeshare system working smoothly, and prevent things from slipping through the cracks. It's also fun to think about those upcoming vacations!

Allowing for spontaneity

We've talked a lot about planning in advance and booking vacations well ahead of time. This level of early preparation often helps you make the most of your timeshare.

Does this mean you can't be spontaneous and take off for a last minute trip? Of course not! Heading off on a spur of the moment trip, or booking a stay at an unusual and unplanned destination, can be exciting and fun.

Jump in and go. There are ways your timeshare can facilitate quick getaways and "I need a break" escapes. For some ideas, see the section *Traveling on short notice*.

Try some wide open searches. Expand your horizons. Search the whole country, or the whole world. When you keep your options open on a very broad search, you're likely to find ideas you never would have thought of otherwise. Maybe the Bahamas weren't on your list to consider, but you discover a place there that sure would make a cool vacation. Look around, and have fun!

14. Potential Ownership Issues

Maintenance fee increases

Just like homes and cars, timeshare resorts need continual maintenance. Your annual maintenance fees cover the cost of cleaning, maintaining, repairing, and managing your property. Maintenance fees are generally higher for more expensive destinations, higher end resorts, and larger units. Most places bill these annually, though some companies do it monthly.

Unfortunately, your timeshare maintenance fees are not fixed, and they go up over time. Hopefully this is in line with inflationary increases, but sometimes the fees rise quite a bit faster. Here's a breakdown of what you need to know about maintenance fees.

Fees support your value. Though you may hate to get your annual maintenance bill, this is actually protecting the value of your timeshare. If they stopped doing maintenance on the resort, pretty soon neither you nor anyone else would want to stay there. Low fees may be nice, but inadequate maintenance can be a problem.

How fees are allocated. In a resort where everyone owns a share of the resort directly, the costs are shared between all of the owners, with your share determined by what you own. The owner of a 2-bedroom would pay more of the maintenance fees than the owner of a studio.

Maintenance fees and seasons. Some places charge owners of high season weeks higher maintenance fees. The idea is that high season units are more valuable, so should pay a greater share of the costs. Some states prohibit charging different fees by season, which means equivalent units pay the same fees, regardless of season. This can lead to a problem situation where low season owners pay more in annual fees than their unit is worth.

Learn more: Seasonal ownership issues. Owning a low season timeshare (or even shoulder season, to a lesser extent), can be problematic. The more seasonal the resort, the bigger this problem can be. This can even end up affecting high season owners in the end. See _Timeshare issues - The Blue Week Blues_, at _TimeshareGame.com/owners-guide-links/_

Maintenance fees with points. When you own points, you may not own a specific resort, but rather part of a larger trust or club that spans multiple resorts. In this situation, the maintenance requirements of the resorts are pooled and shared between all of the owners in that group. Somebody who owns 48,000 points will pay more of the maintenance fees than somebody who owns 22,000.

Normal fee increases. It is normal for the cost of maintenance fees to go up each year, just like the cost of other things in life. Materials, labor, energy costs, and all outsourced components tend to go up with inflation, and that increased cost is passed along to the owners.

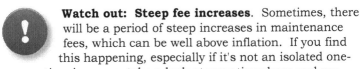

Watch out: Steep fee increases. Sometimes, there will be a period of steep increases in maintenance fees, which can be well above inflation. If you find this happening, especially if it's not an isolated one-time increase, take a look at your timeshare and see what's happening. Compare the fees to other similar properties in the area if you can. Steep fee increases may indicate a problem situation that could get worse and worse. If the fees are unreasonably high, or are trending in that direction, then it could be time to re-evaluate whether you still want to own this timeshare.

There are a number of factors that could lead to steep fee increases. Here are some of the most common reasons.

* **Deferred maintenance adds up**. If a resort has had inadequate maintenance for a period of time, things can get run down. This can mean that you wind up with more

maintenance required later on, and higher than normal fees to cover it.

* **Management increases**. Management companies charge the resort to manage the property. The fee they take for this can vary. If the management company increases their fee (often a percentage of the overall budget), or your resort switches to a new management company, your maintenance fees could go up as a result.

* **Fewer owners**. If your timeshare gets into a situation where multiple owners default on their units, you can wind up with a smaller number of owners to share the maintenance burden. This means higher costs for everyone, until that situation can get turned around.

* **New ownership wants to upgrade**. In some cases, a resort or timeshare company can get into financial difficulties that end with it being bought by another company. This is a complex situation (discussed further in the section *Company mergers and bankruptcies*). One possible outcome is that the new company wants to upgrade the resort, and the burden of paying for this falls onto the existing timeshare owners, resulting in overly high fees.

Who decides about maintenance? The management company is responsible for maintaining the property, and they make recommendations on what has to be done. This company and the developer may be affiliated, or could be two branches of the same company. Generally there is an owner's association, and a board of directors that has to approve the recommendations. Whether this provides effective checks and balances depends on the composition of the board. For more on this, see *Resort ownership and voting rights*.

Special assessments

Special assessments are additional payments to cover large repairs or upgrades that can't be handled through the timeshare's normal maintenance fees and reserve funds.

Nobody wants to see one of these, since it can be a substantial impact to your finances and cost of ownership. The only good thing about a special assessment is that unlike maintenance fees, you only have to pay it once.

Examples of special assessments. If a timeshare resort needs a new roof, or new air conditioning units, or extensive repairs due to deferred maintenance, the costs to handle such an item could be billed as a special assessment to the owners.

How it works with weeks. When your resort needs a major item that's being funded with a special assessment, the total cost is divided among the owners, proportionally based on what they each own. A special assessment might be a few hundred dollars per timeshare, or even a few thousand. This one-time charge will show up on your normal bill, along with your standard maintenance fees. Most assessments are billed in one lump sum, but it's possible for a large assessment to be spread over two or three years.

How it works with points. Say you own points in a resort group with 12 different resorts. If one of these resorts requires significant repairs or upgrades, the cost will be split among the points owners of the entire group of 12 resorts. This makes your share a lot less than if you were a direct owner of the one resort with a problem. On the other hand, it also means you share in the repairs for all 12 resorts, not just one, and may end up paying for repairs at resorts you'll never even see.

With points, you usually won't find these repairs itemized as a special assessment. Instead, the cost will just be rolled into your normal bill. You still pay your share of the cost - it just won't be labeled as a special assessment.

Watch out: Claim that points owners "don't pay special assessments". A common line used to convince weeks owners to convert to points, is to raise the threat of a special assessment, and say that changing to points will allow the owner to avoid that extra cost. This is not really true. Even if you own points, the timeshare owners still pay for repairs at a resort. The developer isn't going to just swallow the cost - it's passed on to the owners.

What can you do? If you're billed for a special assessment, you will have to pay it to continue your right to use the property. If you don't pay on time, you will probably be charged late fees in addition. So what are your options?

- **Accept and pay up**. If the cost isn't too big a burden for you, then it's easiest and best to just accept the extra cost as part of what you pay to vacation there. It's not that different from home ownership - things happen and unexpected costs arise. Hopefully you will end up with a better resort as a result.

- **Sell out**. You can try to sell your timeshare, but this can be difficult with a major assessment pending. Most potential owners won't want to get involved at this time, but if you offer a great price or incentives you may find a buyer.

- **Take it to court**. Filing a lawsuit is another option, but these cases take a lot of work, time and legal fees. Owners in some major cases have gone this route, with mixed results. Unless it's a huge assessment, it's unlikely that a lawsuit is going to be practical.

- **Give it back**. Some companies will let you give a unit back to them in these circumstances. Of course, if you paid $45,000 to buy your timeshare at the full retail price, then you won't want to just give that back and be out your $45,000. On the other hand, if you bought a resale timeshare for $1,000 (as we recommend in _Winning the Timeshare Game - Buying the Bargains_), then giving it back could be better than paying the assessment.

One company in Canada offered owners the choice between paying a $3,000 assessment and keeping their timeshare, or paying $2,000 to have the company take it back. Owners were very upset, but an initial lawsuit upheld the company's right to do this.

- **Get involved**. Becoming active with the owners association will at least keep you in the know about what's happening, though it's unlikely to change anything about a current special assessment.

What happens if you don't pay the fees

If you don't pay maintenance fees and special assessments by the specified due date, it will impact your ability to use your timeshare. If you continue not to pay, you will encounter more serious consequences.

Cannot reserve a vacation. If you are not up to date on all of your fees, you will be unable to make a vacation reservation for your own timeshare. This means that you cannot use it yourself, you cannot trade it, and you cannot rent it out to someone else.

Existing reservations may be at risk. Say you booked a reservation two years in advance, paying the estimated fees for that year at the time. You deposited this with one of the major exchange companies, and used it to book an exchange vacation somewhere else. If you get a second bill for that time period, either a special assessment or an added bill to cover fee increases, you need to pay that in order to keep the reservation you have. If you don't pay the fees, that reservation, and any exchange based on it, could be cancelled.

Collection efforts. If you have not paid your timeshare bills after some period of time, you will find that collection agencies come after you for the money, with harassing letters and phone calls.

Foreclosure as a last step. If you own a deeded timeshare and have not paid your fees for an extended time, then foreclosure is a last step in the process. This means that your timeshare deed will return to the resort, for them to find a new owner. If your timeshare is not deeded, then an official foreclosure may not be needed in order to take over your timeshare.

Your credit takes a hit. Some people may think that not paying for a timeshare until the resort takes it back via foreclosure, is a reasonable way to get rid of an unwanted timeshare. It's not a free ride, however. If your timeshare goes through a foreclosure, your credit rating will take a serious hit, which can affect your interest rates on everything else.

Non-payment in international cases. If you live in one country and own a timeshare in a different country, then what happens when you don't pay your bills? This will depend on the specifics, since every country has their own rules. What happens with collection agencies, foreclosures, and credit reporting will vary by location, so do some research before deciding to stop paying your fees.

Owner's update = More high pressure sales

When you arrive for your timeshare vacation, chances are they will tell you about an "Owner's meeting," "Owner's update," "Annual update," or something similar. If you decide to attend, be prepared for scare tactics, high pressure sales, and money grabs.

You can just skip it. The easiest thing to do is just to skip the meeting. Unless you booked some special deal with strings attached, you are under no obligation to attend the meeting. You will be happier with your timeshare if you don't listen to them tell you that what you own isn't nearly as good as something more expensive. You will be happier with your vacation if you spend your time relaxing and enjoying, not listening to a pushy salesperson.

You can attend, but not buy. If you're curious to hear what they have to say about their latest, greatest program, then you can attend the meeting. Watch out, however. This is usually going to be a high pressure attempt to take money out of your bank account. You can easily end up spending hours there, as they try every trick in the book to get you to pay them more money.

What to expect. Most owner's update meetings are pretty similar to an initial timeshare sales presentation, but with an added scare factor. They will often tell you that whatever you own right now is no good, compared to the new thing they're selling. Then it will be hours of working you, trying tactic after tactic to wear you down, overcome your objections, and scare you into pulling out your checkbook. Don't believe what they say, and don't buy anything.

Watch out: What you own is "worthless." Say you own the rights to use a 1-bedroom unit for one week per year. They may try to tell you that this is worthless, and you need to buy into some new points system to be a real owner now. Balderdash. You still have the exact same rights that you had before, regardless of what they say. They just want to scare you into spending more money.

Watch out: Special assessment threat. They may try to scare you by saying there's an expensive special assessment coming up soon, and the only way to avoid that is to trade in your resort ownership to join their club (for more money, of course). This is a common tactic, and salespeople have been known to say this even when there is no special assessment pending at all. It's also likely that the money they'll want you to pay is more than the assessment itself (if there even really is one).

Watch out: Giving up your deed. If you currently own a deeded unit, they may try to get you to give up your deed so you can be converted into a club member. Of course, you have to pay more money to do this. You lose the value of owning actual deeded property, and you lose your voting rights at your local resort. Without a deed, you end up with just a paper membership and fees to pay. If you ever want to have input into how your resort is run, keep your deed intact.

Watch out: Upgrade to points may be an expensive downgrade. If you own one or more weeks in a company that also does points, they may want to "upgrade" you from weeks to points, or "enroll" you in their points system. Of course, this upgrade costs money. Sometimes this makes sense, but often it doesn't. If you're considering this, take their claims skeptically, and do your own research. You could easily find that you would give up your week, pay more money now, pay more every year for on-going fees, and wind up without enough points to even reserve the week you used to own. That's an expensive downgrade.

Learn more: Shifting numbers at an owner's update. For a real life account of how this worked at one of our recent owner's meetings, and some tips on what to expect, see _Timeshare Owners' Update - Watch the Math_, at _TimeshareGame.com/owners-guide-links/_

Watch out: No numbers available. Sometimes, a salesperson will gloss over exactly how much your new fees would be after you upgrade, or they may claim they don't know exactly how many points it would cost to get a certain vacation you want. Why would you buy something when they can't even tell you exactly what you're getting?

Watch out: Premium benefits can change. Many companies will want to sell you more points, with the promise that after you get to a certain level (Elite, Premiere, Gold, Platinum, etc.), you will receive special benefits. If these benefits are useful for you, then it may be enticing. The problem lies in the fact that the company can change the benefits at any time. Many owners have been upset to find that a benefit they made use of is cut from the system. They paid a lump sum to purchase additional points to reach the elite level, as well as higher maintenance fees every year. Remember - the company can change the rules whenever they want, but you're still stuck with those higher fees.

Don't expect reliable information. As you can see from the list above, don't expect reliable information if you attend an owner update meeting. It's really just an excuse to get you in a room with a salesperson again. Unless you have a specific reason you want to attend, just skip it, and save yourself the headaches.

What if you DO want more points? Even if you do want to buy more timeshare points, attending the owner's meeting is not the best way to get them. This is something that you should research on your own, and decide about in a non-pressured environment, where you can take your time to think it over, and reach a careful decision. For more about adding to your timeshare ownership, see *Your Timeshare Portfolio*.

Resort ownership and voting rights

The owners of a timeshare resort should have some control over the management of the resort and the fees that are charged. However, the picture can get cloudy when you start dealing with trusts and clubs. Here's what you need to know.

Basic scenario with deeded ownership. In this scenario, the resort is owned by all of the timeshare owners, who have deeded interests in the property. There is a Homeowners Association (HOA), which elects a Board of Directors. The board hires the management company, and establishes budgets and fees. All timeshare owners have a right to vote for the board, and on other important matters. The resort rules may include terms like "any assessment more than $xxx must be approved by at least yy% of the owners."

Who votes? In theory, all of the timeshare owners have the right to vote. In practice, many or most of them never vote. When it's a property they may see once a year, if that, most owners don't pay much attention to what's going on. As an owner, you should receive a proxy for voting, but often that just gets tossed in the recycle bin.

Why does it matter? The HOA and board of directors make important decisions about the resort that can affect you. Increasing maintenance fees by 18%? A special assessment bill for $2,000? Changing management companies if they're charging too much or not doing a good job? The HOA and board of directors can decide issues like these. That's why it matters.

Buying into a trust. Rather than owning a resort directly, you may own part of a trust that owns multiple resorts. Say you buy into Company ABC's vacation club, which gives you an ownership in the ABC trust. Now you don't vote at the resort anymore. Instead, you vote for the directors of the ABC trust. The ABC directors then vote their ownership as a bloc when it comes to elections at the resorts.

Combined ownership. A lot of times, a resort may end up with different types of ownership. Some owners bought deeded weeks, and own directly at that resort. Others own points in a vacation club, so their ownership is through a trust arrangement, and they have little control of their votes. In practice, a trust which owns at least 10% of the voting rights can usually control what happens at the resort. Once the ABC trust owns that much voting stock, ABC can call the shots, rather than the individual owners.

Management control. It's easy to see how a management company can end up with a controlling interest in a resort. Theoretically, the homeowner's association decides about hiring the management company. However, when the same company (or one which is closely affiliated) effectively controls the voting rights and board of directors, then it's able to take actions which the individual timeshare owners might not be happy with.

Getting involved. Find out about the homeowner's association for your timeshare, and when the meetings are. Even if you can't attend the meetings in person, you should be able to read the minutes of what happened. You should also be able to vote your proxy even if you're not present.

Practically speaking. If you're happy with how your resort is being run, then it probably doesn't matter much to you what's happening with the HOA and board of directors. If you normally use your unit for exchange, you may not pay any attention to that specific resort. The time may come, though, when they make some decisions that affect you. It's smart to find out what your voting rights are, and exercise them.

Management changes

It's difficult for any timeshare management company to keep everyone happy, since there are conflicting objectives. Some owners are most interested in keeping quality high, while other owners are more concerned with keeping fees low. The management company wants to maintain consistent standards across all of their properties to protect their brand, and they're also in business to make money.

Sometimes, these conflicting interests can lead to enough owner unhappiness that a management change results.

How does management change? There are various reasons and ways that the management at a resort can change. Here are a few scenarios.

- **Resort is sold out, developer leaves**. Usually the resort developer works with an associated management company (often a sister company). The developer stays around until the property is fully built and sold, then leaves, and the management company continues. However, sometimes the management changes when the developer leaves.

- **HOA kicks out management company**. This can happen when enough people in a timeshare HOA are unhappy with the management company. The HOA and their board of directors could decide to replace the current management company with another.

- **Management company pulls out**. This could happen for a number of reasons. Perhaps they're not making enough profit on this location, it no longer fits with their plans, or there is rancor between the company and the HOA. When the time comes to renew their contract, the company could decide not to renew.

What happens next? Whatever the reason, it's up to the HOA to hire a new management company to run the resort. Here are a few possible outcomes.

- **Leave resort group, go independent**. For instance, if your resort was run by company ABC and was part of the ABC timeshare system, then it wouldn't be part of that group anymore. You might pay lower fees, but owners would lose any preferential exchange options within that system. The resort might also attract fewer people to exchange into the property.

- **Switch resort group**. It's possible for a resort to switch affiliations, leaving one group and joining another. Instead of being part of the ABC network, the resort becomes part of the XYZ network. The management styles of the two companies, their fee structures, and the benefits they provide to owners, could be different.

- **Fees go down, perhaps quality too**. If the primary reason for changing management was to bring down costs and maintenance fees, this could be a good thing, saving money for the owners. On the other hand, if not managed well, this could result in deterioration of the property over time. The property could become less desirable, both for owners who want to stay there, and in terms of value for exchanges.

- **Quality goes up, and fees do too**. Perhaps the resort wasn't being maintained to high enough standards before, and that's one of the reasons for changing management. If the resort brings in a new management company who intends to raise the level of quality, that can mean a sharp increase in maintenance fees.

The right that timeshare owners have via their HOA to change the management company is an important one. Making such a move may be a smart decision. However, changing companies can be a big deal so it's not something to enter into lightly.

Company mergers and bankruptcies

Just like other businesses, timeshare companies can come and go. Some do well, others struggle financially or even fall into bankruptcy. The strong buy out the weak, the big buy out the small. Mergers and acquisitions can mean that the company you bought into, isn't the same company you end up owning with a few years later.

Bankruptcy, deeded timeshares. As long as you own a deeded timeshare, or own in a vacation club where you own part of a trust that holds the deeds, then you own something real that will continue after the company goes bankrupt. What normally happens in this case is that a different company will come in, buy any unsold inventory, and take over management of the resort. Due to the amount of inventory they own, the new company will often have enough voting rights to control the board.

Watch out: Bankruptcy of a non-deeded vacation club. If you bought into a non-deeded vacation club, then all you own is a piece of paper saying you have the right to use the club. If the vacation club company goes under, you could be left with nothing. This is the worst case scenario, and it's one reason why it's good to own a deeded timeshare. On the other hand, if you wanted to get out of this timeshare, that could be the silver lining. You would no longer be responsible for maintenance fees, but the money you spent on the purchase would be lost.

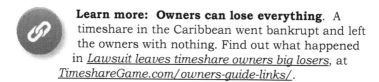

Learn more: Owners can lose everything. A timeshare in the Caribbean went bankrupt and left the owners with nothing. Find out what happened in *Lawsuit leaves timeshare owners big losers*, at *TimeshareGame.com/owners-guide-links/*.

Your rights in mergers and buyouts. If you own a timeshare with company ABC, which then merges into company XYZ, your ownership will continue, though things may change. If you have an annual 1-week, 1-bedroom unit, then you will still have the same thing. If you own points that give you certain occupancy rights, then you still have the same rights. You'll just go through a different company to use your timeshare. It can get confusing (and they may purposely make it more so), but your contractual rights will persist after the acquisition. (Note the bankruptcy exception to this mentioned above.)

Management changes. Everything in the section above about management changes can apply here too, when the management of the resort is changed as a result of a merger, acquisition, or bankruptcy. The new company could have different quality standards, fees, processes, and owner benefits, than the old company had. You might end up being happy with the changes, or not.

Converting to the new system. You're sure to be asked to various Owner Meetings, Transition Meetings, etc. where the new company tries to sell you on converting or "upgrading" to their system. They'll probably use scare tactics, telling you that what you own is useless now (not true). It's also a sure bet that they will want you to pay more money for the privilege of "upgrading," even if they're giving you a horrible deal. Be extremely wary of anything you're told, and don't believe all the scary things you hear.

Be prepared. Read the earlier section, *Owner's update = More high pressure sales*, to learn what to watch out for. Don't let them scare you into taking a bad deal, giving up your deed, or paying far too much money. Don't let them rush you into an ill advised transaction. There's no reason you need to decide on the spot. They may say "This deal is only good today," but they say that every day. Take your time, and make a thoughtful decision.

Let the dust settle. There's usually a period of some confusion, as operations are transitioned from one company to another. Once things settle down, you'll be in a better position to decide what to do. Give it a chance, and see how things look once the new company is in charge for awhile.

Decide later. Once things have settled down, you can make an informed decision. You may find that you like the new company, and are happy with the changes. You may decide that you want to switch to the new company's point system instead of your current ownership. Or you may find that you're not very happy with the changes they're making, and decide to get out. If so, it will generally be easier to sell your timeshare once all of the questions surrounding the transition are settled, because few buyers will want to purchase a timeshare while it's in the middle of a major upheaval.

The end of a timeshare's life

When you own a deeded piece of property, whether a timeshare or otherwise, you usually own it in perpetuity. Most timeshare contracts are written so that they last forever, or at least until you sell the timeshare or pass away. There are, however, some ways in which a timeshare can cease to exist.

Contracts with an expiration date. Some timeshare contracts, usually Right to Use contracts, have a preset expiration date. For instance, when you buy the timeshare, it might have an expiration date 25 years in the future, so you are buying the right to use that timeshare for 25 years. As time goes by, if you sell this to someone else, they might be buying a contract with just 10 years left, or even 5. When the expiration date arrives, your contract terminates. You no longer have any right to use this timeshare anymore. Your obligation to make payments ceases at the same time, which in some cases is a good thing.

Property ceases to be a timeshare. If you own a deeded week at a specific resort, this is a situation that's unusual, but it does happen occasionally. What happens is that the owners, via the HOA and board of directors, vote to disband the timeshare. Provisions for this to happen may be written into the original timeshare documents.

An example where this could happen is if you have an older timeshare in a great location by the beach. The timeshare has been there for 30 years or more, while the property around it continued to be developed. As an aging timeshare, the units have little value and are hard to sell. However, if the entire property was sold to a developer, then owners could recoup more money than they would trying to sell their timeshares, especially the owners of less desirable off-season weeks. If the entire property is sold, then the proceeds should be split between all of the owners, according to what they own.

Another example could be if an independent timeshare resort was catastrophically damaged by a natural event such as a hurricane or earthquake. While the property should certainly be insured, there may be nobody who wants to undertake the complicated and expensive job of rebuilding it. The owners may decide to just sell the property instead.

Leaving a timeshare in your will

If you own a deeded timeshare, then you can leave it to your heirs, just like any other piece of real estate. Before you do that, here are some things you need to think about.

Deeded vs. Right to Use. If you own a Deeded timeshare, then this is a piece of real property, and you can pass it on as an inheritance. If you own a Right to use timeshare, then you can probably still do this, but you need to check your contract.

What's it worth? Look into the resale value of your timeshare, and you'll probably find that it's not worth much on the resale market. Sure, you may have paid $50,000 for this and get wonderful vacations at a beautiful resort, but that doesn't mean your heirs could sell it for nearly that much.

Some high demand timeshares with limited competition, like top tier resorts or fixed weeks during the holidays, can command reasonable resale prices, though usually these are still well below the original retail cost. Off season weeks, areas with high inventory, and less desirable resorts, may sell for as little as $1. It's sad, but true.

What's the obligation? If you pass your timeshare on to your heirs, you're also passing along the obligation for the annual maintenance fees. Say your annual maintenance fee is $1,000. Will that fit easily into their annual vacation budget, or would that cost be a burden to them?

Would they use it and enjoy it? Have you been to this resort with your kids or grandkids, so that they have fond memories of vacationing there with you? Are they already timeshare owners, who understand how to use and enjoy timeshares? Either of those factors would be positive indications that they would enjoy having your timeshare, assuming they can afford the on-going financial obligation.

On the other hand, if your relatives don't normally have much time or money for holidays, or if they spend every vacation camping in the mountains or cruising on their sailboat, then they might not get much use out of your timeshare.

They can decline it. Estate and probate laws vary by location, but in the US, the heirs can always refuse to accept a deed to a property (unless there was a Joint Tenants deed to start with, in which case someone is already a joint owner). Nobody can force them to inherit the property and take on the associated fees. If your beneficiaries refuse to accept the property, then once the estate is settled, the deed is nullified.

Talk to an expert. If you're considering leaving a timeshare in your will, think about it carefully to see if this will be a good thing for your beneficiaries. Maybe it will be a great thing for them, maybe not. If you decide to proceed, then get expert advice from a lawyer who knows this field. There could be complications, especially if there are multiple states or countries involved.

Expert tip: Sell it and leave them the money. If your heirs can't comfortably afford the cost of the timeshare fees, or won't be able to make good use of it, then if you leave them the timeshare, they will either have to refuse it (losing all value) or accept it and sell it (which is complicated for them). Since you know more about this timeshare than they do and already have clear title in your name, it will be easier for you to sell it yourself. This way, you can leave them the cash proceeds as a nice bequest.

Beneficiaries should get a lawyer as well. If you receive a timeshare as a beneficiary of someone else's will, then it's also wise to seek a lawyer. Do your own research into the resale value and annual costs of the timeshare, to see whether you really want to accept it. If you choose to refuse the bequest and decline the timeshare, then a lawyer can help you make sure the necessary paperwork is completed, so that you don't end up with an unwanted obligation.

15. Your Timeshare Portfolio

Once you get the hang of timeshares and discover how much use you can get out of one, you may choose to expand your holdings by buying one or more additional timeshares. This is quite a common situation among people who know how to play the game and make the most of their timeshares. If you're considering adding to your timeshare portfolio, there are things you need to think about.

Staying in one system vs. diversifying

A key consideration is whether you should stick with one company, or diversify and buy something different. There are pros and cons.

Advantages of expanding what you already own

* **You know the system**. This can be a significant advantage, though not a permanent one. If you've owned in one system for a few years, you have had time to figure out the tricks. You know how the reservation dates work, how borrowing or saving points works, and how to use your timeshare for exchanges. If you buy into a different system, you'll have to learn this again as you figure it out for a different timeshare.

* **Elite status levels**. Depending on what you currently own and what you want to purchase, buying more with the same company may move you into an elite status level - silver, gold, platinum, etc. Before you make this an important criteria, make sure to verify whether buying resale will convey the elite status, or whether you'd have to pay the full retail price to get that. You need to know whether the elite benefits you get are worth the purchase price you have to pay. Usually it is very difficult for the added benefits to pay off financially if you're paying full price for additional timeshare points.

* **May be more cost effective**. Depending on the fee structure for your timeshares, sometimes the fees are

spread more effectively when you own more with the same company. For instance, if there's a fixed $299 fee to belong to a vacation club, plus a maintenance fee cost per point, the total annual cost per point ends up being less if you own more points. If you own just 2,000 points, the fixed cost adds almost 15 cents per point to your costs. If you expand that to 20,000 points, the fixed cost is only 1.5 cents per point.

Watch out: Buying more points is not cheaper. The above calculation is one that you're likely to hear referenced in an owner's meeting. The salesperson may tell you that buying more points makes it cheaper. It does in a way, in that the fixed cost is less per point. However, remember that your total cost and annual payment obligation will be going up with more points, not down.

* **It's the easiest thing to do**. Whenever you visit your timeshare, the salespeople will (of course), want you to expand your holdings with them. They make it easy, too. You don't need to do a lot of research and due diligence, because you already know what you have. Just sign a check, and you're done (if you want to buy at full retail price, that is)!

Advantages of buying something different

* **Different set of resorts**. Buying into a different company can get you preferred access to their resorts. For instance, if you already own Hilton, you could buy a Marriott timeshare in order to get into Marriott resorts you cannot access with your Hilton. This could be a consideration if your current company doesn't have anything in an area where you want to vacation.

* **Different exchange company**. If your timeshare is associated with RCI or Interval International, then buying a different timeshare could get you access to the other exchange company's inventory. This can give you a greater set of exchange options, and also a better selection of

getaways and extra vacations. There is a learning curve with this, however, as you learn how to use another company effectively.

* **Splitting points for resale**. If you've added points to a single account over time, and end up with a million points, can you split it up when you're selling, or would you need to sell it in one lump to a buyer? Verify the rules before you get in too deep. If you're trying to sell a big pool of points, you will find a limited number of buyers who are willing to purchase that many points at once. It also makes it difficult to scale down when you no longer want to vacation as much.

* **You may become disenchanted**. People can fall out of love with timeshare companies over time. Perhaps they've been raising the annual fees too quickly. Perhaps they discontinued certain elite benefits you had come to rely on. Perhaps they're changing some other rule in a way that you're unhappy with. Whatever the reason, if you become disenchanted with a company, you'll be happier if all your timeshare eggs aren't in that basket.

Weeks vs. points vs. both

The ins and outs of weeks and points were discussed in the section *Weeks, Points, and Hybrid systems*. The question now is whether it makes sense to focus all of your timeshare portfolio on one side or the other, or whether it makes more sense to have some of each.

Both weeks and points have their fervent supporters, who believe their choice is the only way to go. Typically, proponents of weeks like the security of having a deeded week, which cannot be changed at the whim of a timeshare company. Proponents of points usually cite the increased flexibility of points as the big advantage, and see that as the way of the future.

Unless you're already a die hard supporter of one side or the other, there are reasons to consider both for your timeshare portfolio. Here are a few things to consider.

Floating weeks let you work the system. When you have points, you get a certain number of points and that's it. You can spend them however you choose, but what you get is fixed. Floating weeks generally give you more control, because in most systems, you can vary how much trading power you get by reserving the best weeks. If you pay attention and work the system, this can be a good thing. If you don't, it can be a disadvantage.

Some resorts are better in weeks, others in points. There are anomalies in the exchange company systems, which sometimes value a particular resort more highly in weeks than in points, while other places get the opposite. In Interval, you cannot see the trading power, but in RCI you can see both the points and the trading power for a week. It's worth noting that this is not necessarily a permanent advantage, since RCI may change either TPU or points allocations sometime in the future.

Expert tip: Comparing a resort in RCI weeks and points. If you're considering buying at a resort that does both RCI weeks and points, or if you already own a week and are considering changing it to points, it's worth taking a look at how they compare before you make a decision. You can use the online Resort Directory to view the points charts, and the Deposit Calculator to view the TPUs. Here are a couple of examples:

▸ Tahoe Beach & Ski Club: Week 33, 1-bedroom = 23 TPUs or 36,000 points = 1,565 points per TPU

▸ Grandview Las Vegas: Week 33, 2-bedroom = 17 TPUs or 98,000 points = 5,765 points per TPU

The two examples above show an enormous difference in their relative valuations in points vs. TPUs. Grandview gets more than three times as many points per TPU as the Tahoe resort does. With these two, it makes more sense to own the Tahoe Beach & Ski Club as a week, and Grandview Las Vegas as points.

Owning both gives maximum flexibility. When you own different things, you get access to multiple pools of vacation inventory, and multiple ways to work the system to get what you want. This additional flexibility is probably the biggest advantage to owning some weeks and some points.

Owning both can be the most complicated. There are pros and cons to everything, and this is the downside to all that flexibility. The more different things you own, the more complicated it is to learn how to use them all most effectively, and the more difficult it is to plan and track all of your timeshare activities. How much energy do you want to put into this? Variety is more powerful, but simple is easier.

Scaling up and down as needed

As you move through life, your family and work situations change, and so do your vacation needs. Here are a few common situations.

- You buy your first timeshare for family travel, but eventually the kids grow up and move away.

- You have limited vacation time during your career years, but then retire and have time to travel much more.

- Your financial priorities change, and you want to spend your money on something else besides timeshare travel.

Whatever the reasons, just recognize that you may want to scale your timeshare portfolio up and down over the years. This is a consideration when you are wondering what to buy next.

Buying and selling weeks. When you're dealing with timeshare weeks, the idea of scaling up and down is fairly straight forward. You can buy individual weeks at whatever resorts you want, and end up with however many you want to own. When the time comes to scale back, you select which week or weeks you want to sell.

Buying and selling points, different companies. In this scenario, you buy points in multiple companies. You might end up owning some Worldmark points, some Wyndham points, and some Shell Vacations Club points. When you want to scale back, you could sell any one of these and keep the other two.

Buying and selling points, same company. This is a bit more complicated, since it depends on the specific company rules, and nothing is as simple as you'd think.

▸ When you purchase more points to add to your account, will they wind up with the same anniversary and expiration dates as those you already own? Will buying in a different trust or use year complicate this?

▸ If you end up with both resale and developer points, will you end up with different rules for each?

▸ Will you be able to split the points in your account later, to sell just some of them when you want to scale down?

Make sure you understand the rules for your company well before investing in additional timeshare points with them. The rules you have for your existing points might be a bit different for added points.

Liquidity, or lack thereof

When you buy a timeshare, you are taking on an obligation to keep paying maintenance fees for the rest of your life, until the end of the contract, or until you sell the timeshare to someone else. You have your initial purchase price + your annual maintenance fees tied up with this timeshare until you are able to sell it. The bottom line is that timeshares are not very liquid.

Don't expect to get your money back. This is especially true if you bought from the developer at retail prices. If you paid full price for a timeshare, don't think you will be able to sell it for that. In order to get rid of the timeshare and your on-going financial obligation, you will probably have to settle for far less than what you paid.

Some timeshares are harder to sell than others. Some do retain some value, and can be sold on a site like eBay or Redweek without taking very long. Other timeshares can be difficult to get rid of, and you might have these posted for sale for some time without getting a bite.

If you need to sell fast, lower the price. The lower your asking price, the more attractive your offering, and the more likely it is to sell quickly. If you paid a lot of money to buy your timeshare and are hoping to get some of your money back, you probably won't want to sell it for a bargain, but keeping your price high can slow the sale. On the other hand, if you bought resale for a cheap price, and your goal is to reduce your maintenance fee burden, then you can lower the asking price without losing much money.

Sometimes you need to give it away. In some cases, the only way to get rid of a timeshare is to sell it for $1 or give it away for free. You might even need to sweeten the deal with a prepaid year of maintenance fees. This is especially true if you own at a problem property, where fees are too high, the property seems rundown, or there is a big special assessment in the works. Off season weeks are also sometimes a problem when the maintenance fees are too high for the value.

Learn more: Problems with owning off-season weeks. It can be quite challenging to sell a timeshare if you own an off-season week. Find out more about this at *Timeshare issues - The Blue Week Blues*, at *TimeshareGame.com/owners-guide-links/*

Buying the bargains

The liquidity discussion in the previous section leads right back to buying the bargains when you get a timeshare.

- **If you buy at a low price**, then you can afford to sell at a good price too, which helps you get rid of your timeshare relatively quickly.

- **If you buy at full retail price**, then you either need to take a big financial hit when you sell, take a long time to sell your timeshare, or perhaps both.

Expert tip: Read the buyer's guide. Before you purchase another timeshare, read our companion book "_Winning the Timeshare Game - Buying the Bargains._" This book has a wealth of advice on what to consider in making a buying decision, how to select and research a timeshare, and how to find and evaluate the best deals. It could save you a lot of money, and headaches, too!

Playing the game to win

Making the most of your timeshare really is like playing a game. It's a complex game with changing rules, but it's also one that has some great payoffs. Practice makes perfect, and the more time you spend exploring your timeshare options, looking at your exchange possibilities, and learning the ins and outs of the rules for your timeshare, the better you will be positioned in the game.

When you can score an incredible vacation exchange, or learn how to rent your timeshare for more than your maintenance fees, you get a great sense of accomplishment, as well as the tangible benefits.

As you begin to master the game, working with timeshares becomes more fun. Many people at this stage decide to expand their portfolio, so that they have even more pieces in the game to work with. You'll need to decide what is right for you and your family. In the meantime, have fun in your adventures with the timeshare game!

Learn more: Get timeshare tips, tactics and news. For the latest news, updates, and deals in the world of timeshares, you'll find regular updates on our blog. Check it out at _Winning the Timeshare Game, TimeshareGame.com_. You can also sign up for free updates, and get the latest news and articles delivered straight to your inbox.

16. Additional Resources

Organizations and resources

Timeshare industry organizations

ARDA (American Resort Development Association) -- (US) A national organization for the US timeshare industry, which advocates for policies that promote the growth of the industry. *arda.org*

ATHOC (Australian Timeshare and Holiday Ownership Council) -- (Australia) This organization represents the timeshare industry in Australia, and works to promote industry best practices. They also offer information and support to timeshare owners. *athoc.com.au*

CRDA (Canadian Resort Development Association) -- (Canada) The national organization in Canada, created to encourage and maintain a high standard of ethical conduct throughout the industry. Works with the ARDA on various initiatives. *crda.com*

ROC (Resort Owners' Coalition) -- (US) Affiliated with the ARDA, this is an alliance of over a million timeshare owners, developers and managers. They propose and support legislative and regulatory policies. If you own a timeshare in the US, you can expect to see a "voluntary contribution" to this organization added to your yearly bill. *arda-roc.org*

RDO (Resort Development Organisation) -- (Europe) The trade association for vacation ownership across Europe, made of up of developers, exchange and management companies, and more. The purpose is to promote vacation ownership, protect the interests of the timeshare industry and owners, and target fraudulent activity that harms timeshare owners. Formerly called the OTE (Organisation for Timeshare in Europe). *rdo.org*

TATOC (The Association of Timeshare Owners Committees) -- (Europe) Run by timeshare owners for timeshare owners, this organization was created to safeguard and enhance the timeshare holiday experience for existing and prospective owners, and to be the voice of owners. The largest consumer association for timeshare owners in Europe, they have a consumer help line to aid in problem situations. _tatoc.co.uk_

Timeshare exchange companies

DAE (Dial An Exchange) -- Worldwide independent timeshare exchange company, not affiliated with specific resorts like RCI or II. Free basic membership or paid premium memberships. _daelive.com_

Hawaii Timeshare Exchange (HTSE) -- Independent timeshare exchange company that specializes in Hawaii, but also covers mainland US and some international locations. Paid membership. _htse.net_

Interval International -- The second largest timeshare exchange network, with thousands of resorts worldwide. To use this, your timeshare resort must be affiliated with Interval International. Paid membership. _intervalworld.com_

Platinum Interchange -- Independent timeshare exchange company, not affiliated with specific resorts. The third largest exchange company. Free membership. _platinuminterchange.com_

RCI (Resort Condominiums International) -- The largest timeshare exchange company, with over 4,000 resorts around the world. To use this, your timeshare resort must be affiliated with RCI. Paid membership. _rci.com_

SFX Preferred Resorts -- Independent timeshare exchange company, specializing in highly rated resorts. Free basic membership or paid premium membership. _sfx-resorts.com_

Timeshare Juice -- Site that lets you exchange your timeshare directly with other owners. Free membership. _timesharejuice.com_

Trading Places International -- Independent timeshare exchange company. Handles resorts worldwide, but specializes in US and Mexico. Free basic membership or paid premium membership. *tradingplaces.com*

Vacation Point Exchange -- An online forum for people to exchange timeshare points in different companies (Disney, Marriott, and others). Free membership. *vacationpointexchange.com*

VRI*ety -- An exchange network for owners of properties that are associated with VRI. Free for VRI owners. *vrietyexchange.com*

Useful websites

eBay -- An online auction site where people sell everything under the sun, including timeshares (both sales and rentals). *ebay.com*

Redweek -- A site focused on timeshare sales and rentals. Owners can post their own timeshares for sale or rent, and potential buyers or renters can connect with them directly, with no middlemen or commissions. The site also provides resort reviews, a blog, and a forum. Basic membership is free, or you can pay $14.99/year for full access. *redweek.com*

TUG (Timeshare Users' Group) -- An online user's group for people who own timeshares. There is an active forum, timeshare reviews, and a marketplace for buying, selling or renting timeshares. The $15/year membership fee is well worth it if you are active in timeshares. *tug2.net*

Winning the Timeshare Game -- The website associated with this book. The site contains information useful for timeshare owners and buyers, and is updated frequently with more timeshare news and tips. *timesharegame.com*

Timeshare glossary

Accommodation certificate (AC): A credit you get that is good for a stay at a resort. Interval International members may receive an AC good at specific locations, during a specific timeframe. No timeshare exchange is required, just a reservation fee, which varies on different offers.

Accelerated use: A right to use program which allows a timeshare owner to use their vacation time more rapidly than normal. For instance, if you would normally have annual usage, you could take two or more vacations in a year rather than waiting until they would normally be available.

Accrued weeks: Weeks that you carried over from a prior year, which are available for use during the current year.

Affiliated resort: Most timeshare resorts are part of a group of affiliated resorts, often built by the same developer or part of the same vacation club. Owners at one resort have preferential rights to use other affiliated resorts in the group.

All inclusive (AI): All inclusive resorts charge you a certain amount per person that covers all of your food, beverages, and activities while you stay there. At some places this is mandatory, at other places it's optional.

Annual: With an annual timeshare, you have the right to use your timeshare every year. This is the most common arrangement.

ARDA (American Resort Development Association): A trade association for the US timeshare industry, which lobbies for policies that support the industry.

Bank: If you choose not to use your timeshare at your home resort, you can bank it with one of the exchange companies. You then have this available as a credit to exchange for a stay at a different resort.

Biennial: You have the right to use the resort every other year, as opposed to Annual, where you can use the resort every year. Also called Every other year (EOY), Even years, or Odd years.

Bonus time: The ability to reserve extra nights at your home timeshare, when space is available, at preferential owner rates.

BR: Short for bedroom. Timeshare units are usually either Hotel (no kitchen), Studio (one room with bed, sitting area and kitchenette), 1BR (one bedroom, with separate living room and kitchen), or 2BR (two bedrooms, with separate living room and kitchen).

Check in date: The most typical arrangement for timeshare weeks is a 7-day stay. Some resorts offer Saturday to Saturday, others will have Friday to Friday, Sunday to Sunday, or sometimes a different day. If you have a Saturday to Saturday week, then your check-in date is Saturday, even if you don't show up until Monday.

Closing costs: When you buy a timeshare there are typically certain costs associated with closing the deal. This can include deed preparation, recording fee, escrow fee, transfer fee, and administrative charges.

Club membership / Trust membership: A type of timeshare system where rather than owning a portion of a resort directly, you buy a membership to a club. The resort facilities are controlled by trustees, and your membership gives you a right to use the resort. Sometimes the trust is backed by deeds, sometimes not.

Cooling off period: Also called a Rescission period, this is a legally mandated time during which you can change your mind after buying a timeshare. It is designed to protect consumers who are pressured into making a bad purchase. The length of time you have to rescind your contract varies from place to place, depending on local laws.

DAE (Dial An Exchange): An independent timeshare exchange company.

Deed: A legal document that proves ownership of a property. If you own a deeded timeshare, then you have a deed to it, just like a home or other piece of real estate.

Deeded property: A piece of real estate with a deed that establishes the ownership. With a deeded timeshare, you have a deed to the specific property you own, typically one week per year in a certain type of unit. The deed is recorded with the appropriate government agency. Just like owning other real estate, you can sell it, rent it, or leave it for your heirs. Also called Fee simple.

Deeded trust: A vacation club where the trustees hold deeds to the property. The timeshare owners don't own a portion of the resort, instead they own a portion of the trust and a membership in the club, which gives them the right to use the resort. Not all vacation clubs have deeded trusts - some are not backed by deeds.

Destination club: Another term for Vacation club.

DVC: Disney Vacation Club.

EOY (Every Other Year): A timeshare that gives you the right to use the unit every other year. Same as Biennial.

Escrow: A secure system for arranging real estate purchases, where a trusted third party holds the buyer's funds during the closing period. Once the paperwork is done and the sale is finalized, the funds are released from escrow to the seller.

Exchange: Trading your timeshare at the resort you own, for a vacation at a different resort. There are several timeshare exchange companies that facilitate these trades.

Exchange company: A company which allows individual timeshare owners to deposit (or bank) their timeshare, making it available for exchange with other timeshare owners at different resorts. The largest exchange companies are RCI and Interval International (II).

Exchange fee: A transaction fee that you pay for processing a timeshare exchange.

Fee simple: Another term for deeded ownership, in which the timeshare owner actually has a deed to the property.

Fixed unit: A form of timeshare ownership where you own a specific unit at the resort, for a specific time period each year. For instance, you might own a week in unit #1714, and when you visit your resort each year, you always get that same unit.

Fixed week: A type of timeshare ownership where you own a specific week of the year at your resort. The weeks are numbered starting with 1 at the start of the year. If you own week 19, then you get to use your timeshare the 19th week of each year. This could be combined with a fixed unit (e.g. unit #1714 in week 19 each year), or it could be a certain type of unit (e.g. a 2-bedroom unit in week 19 each year).

Floating: With a floating timeshare, you don't own a specific week at a resort, you own an interval of use that can float from week to week each year. At most resorts, the year is split into high, medium and low seasons, depending on demand. Owners purchase a floating week in a particular season. For example, you own a floating week in high season, which you can schedule anytime within that season. It is subject to availability, since you are competing for a given week with other owners who bought the same season. Some places consider the entire year to be high season, so your week can float throughout the year.

Fractional ownership: A timeshare arrangement where you own a fraction of a vacation property. Typically this term is applied in cases where you own more than one week per year at a resort.

Guest certificate: If you want to let someone else use your timeshare, or a timeshare vacation you got through an exchange or purchased as an extra vacation, you can do this by getting them a guest certificate from the resort or exchange company.

HGVC: Hilton Grand Vacation Club.

Holiday club: Another term for Vacation club.

Holiday ownership: Another term for timeshare ownership.

Home group: This is the group of resorts affiliated with your home resort. For instance, if you own a VRI timeshare, your home group includes a list of other VRI resorts. Usually, you get preferential booking rights within your home group.

Home Owners' Association (HOA): With deeded timeshares, the resort is owned by all of the individual timeshare owners. The Home Owners' Association is responsible for decisions about how to run the resort, and owners can elect the board of directors and vote on important issues. Typically the HOA contracts with a management company that handles the day to day operations.

Home resort: Usually (with the exception of some vacation clubs), your timeshare is purchased for a specific home resort. If you have a deeded timeshare, this is the resort listed on the deed. Your timeshare lets you stay at your home resort with no exchange necessary. Usually you have preferential rights at your home resort, such as the ability to make reservations earlier than other people.

Interval: A period of time for which you own a timeshare. The most typical interval is one week per year. This can be further narrowed to a specific interval, such as week 35. The dates for each week are defined on the resort's interval calendar.

Interval calendar: A yearly calendar which shows when each week starts and ends. For example, if a resort counts their weeks Saturday to Saturday (the day of week varies by resort), then week 1 begins on the first Saturday of the year, week 2 on the second Saturday, etc. Normally the year would include 52 weeks, but on years with 53 Saturdays, you end up with 53 weeks.

Interval International (II): The second largest timeshare exchange company, with thousands of affiliated resorts worldwide.

Lease / Leasehold: Rather than owning property outright, there is a long term lease to the property, and you purchase the right to use your timeshare during that time. Whereas a deeded property is yours forever, a lease has an expiration date. For instance, you might have a right to use lease contract which expires after 25 years. In some states and countries deeded ownership is not allowed, so timeshares are all handled as leaseholds.

Levy: A levy is a fee that you need to pay. This could be an annual fee, or a special charge to cover major costs. See Special assessment.

Lock-off / Lock-out unit: A large timeshare unit, which can be split into separate pieces that can be used, rented, or exchanged individually. For instance, a 2-bedroom unit that could be split into a 1-bedroom unit + a studio unit, each of which has its own kitchen and bathroom facilities, and its own keyed external entrance. Owning a lock-off unit provides the owner with flexibility for how to use it.

Maintenance fee (MF): When you buy a timeshare, you are responsible for paying an annual maintenance fee, which covers cleaning, maintenance, repairs, and management of the resort. The total cost of these items is split between all of the timeshare owners, and you receive an annual bill for your portion. Property taxes or club membership fees may also be bundled into the maintenance fee.

Management company: The management company is paid to handle the daily operation of the resort. Often, this is a company closely affiliated with the developer.

Maximum occupancy / Private occupancy: Each timeshare unit has a maximum number of people who can stay there. If you see a unit labeled "Occupancy 4/2," that means the maximum occupancy is 4 people, the private occupancy (in a closed bedroom) is 2 people, and the other 2 are non-private, typically on a pull-out sofa.

MVCI: Marriott Vacation Club International.

Points: A system of timeshare ownership where rather than owning a week at a specific resort, you buy a number of points. (Note - In some hybrid systems, you own an underlying week which is allocated a certain number of points.) You can then spend these points to get vacation time at various resorts in the same points system. You are not tied to a 7-night stay. Your points might buy you 10 nights at a lower priced resort, or 5 nights at a higher priced resort.

Points for deposit (PFD): RCI's program where you can deposit a timeshare week into your RCI points account instead of the normal RCI weeks account.

RCI (Resort Condominiums International): RCI is the largest timeshare exchange company in the world, with over 4,000 resorts in 100 countries.

Red week: Companies often use color coding to signify which weeks of the year are high, medium, or low season. Different companies use different color schemes, but red is a common designation for high season, so a red week is a week during the prime season at that resort.

Resale: If you buy a resale timeshare, you are buying a previously owned timeshare. The first owner buys a timeshare directly from the developer. When they sell it to the next owner, it becomes a resale.

Rescission period: Also called a Cooling off period. This is a legally mandated period during which you can change your mind about a timeshare purchase you made. The intent is to protect consumers from high pressure sales tactics which are common in timeshare presentations. You can cancel (rescind) your contract during that time period with no financial impact. The number of days in your rescission period varies by country and state, and some jurisdictions have no rescission period at all.

Right to use (RTU): With a right to use timeshare, you don't actually have any deeded ownership in a resort. Instead, you have a contract that gives you a right to use the resort for a specific amount of time each year. This type of contract can have an expiration date, unlike a deeded unit.

Season: Most resorts divide the year into different seasons, depending on the demand for each season. At a ski resort, winter months may be high season, while at a beach resort, the summer months are high season. It costs you more to buy, rent, or exchange for a resort during high season than low season. Often there are color codes for the seasons, which can vary by company.

SFX: San Francisco Exchange, an independent timeshare exchange company.

Special assessment: When a resort needs major repairs or upgrades that are not covered by the annual maintenance fees, the additional costs may be billed to the resort owners as a special assessment. This is a charge that's over and above your normal annual fees.

SVC: Shell Vacation Club.

SVN: Starwood Vacation Network.

Timeshare: A system of vacation ownership in which you own the right to use a portion of a vacation resort for a portion of the year. A typical arrangement is owning one week per year, in a certain type of unit, at a certain resort. Depending on the system, you may actually own a portion of the resort (a deeded timeshare), or you may just own the right to use the unit. Some timeshare systems sell you points rather than a fixed interval, and then you exchange your points for a stay at a resort.

Trading power: When you deposit your timeshare with an exchange company, it has a certain trading power based on the location, resort, unit type, dates, and how far in advance you deposit it. Your possible exchanges are limited to other units that have equal or lesser trading power compared with what you have.

Trading Power Unit (TPU): A measurement used by RCI when exchanging units at one resort for another. You may see it called Trading Power, or abbreviated to TPU. When you deposit your timeshare with RCI, you receive a certain number of TPUs for it, which varies depending on how desirable your resort, unit and time period are. You can then exchange for other timeshares that require the same number of TPUs or less.

Triennial: You have the rights to use your timeshare every third year, as opposed to Annual, where you can use the timeshare every year.

TUG (Timeshare Users' Group): An online site with a forum where timeshare owners share information. Members are sometimes referred to as tuggers.

Undivided interest (UDI): In some systems, you purchase an undivided interest in a property. Rather than owning a specific unit or a specific week, you own a non-specific small percentage of the property.

Vacation club: A type of timeshare system where rather than owning a portion of a resort directly, you buy a membership to a club. The resort property itself is controlled by trustees, and your membership gives you a right to use the resorts in that club.

Vacation ownership: Another term for timeshare ownership.

Vacation ownership interval (VOI): The period of time you own, typically one week per year of timeshare ownership.

WM: Worldmark Vacation Club.

Acknowledgements and credits

Image credits

All images are licensed under Creative Commons for Commercial Use.

Cover: Calendar - *Joe Lanman*
    Beach resort - Deanna Keahey
    Beach chair - *Mandolin*
    Chess game - *Tristan Martin*

Introduction: Start button - *Norlando Pobre*
    I love spreadsheets - *Craig Chew-Moulding*

Chapter 1, You've Got Options: Signposts - *Nicola*

Chapter 2, Understanding What You Own:
    Schoolroom - *The shopping sherpa*
    Unit floor plan - *Urbane Apartments*

Chapter 3, Option A - Using Your Timeshare: Swimming pool
- *Dannyqu*
    On the phone - *Garry Knight*

Chapter 4, Option A1 - Using Your Week: Calendar - *Joe Lanman*

Chapter 5, Option A2 - Using Your Points: Price list - *Edward Simpson*
    Expiration dates - *Kate Ter Haar*

Chapter 6, Option B - Exchanging Your Timeshare: Fair trade
- *Lily*

Chapter 7, Option B1 - Exchanging with RCI:
    Wordle for RCI - Deanna Keahey

Chapter 8, Option B2 - Exchanging with Interval:
    Wordle for II - Deanna Keahey

Chapter 9, Option C - Multiplying Your Vacations:
Calculations - *Alan Levine*

Chapter 10, Option D - Taking Fewer Vacations: For rent -
Jen

Chapter 11, Advanced Tactics & Evaluating Options: Chess -
Pen Waggener

Chapter 12, How the Finances Work: Accounting - *o5com*

Chapter 13, Creating Your Timeshare Calendar:
Planning calendar - *Nomadic Lass*
Gears - *DanielSTL*

Chapter 14, Potential Ownership Issues: Rising costs -
Stockmonkeys.com

Chapter 15, Your Timeshare Portfolio: Birdhouses - *See-ming Lee*

Chapter 16, Additional Resources: Bookshelf - *Patrick Hoesly*

Acknowledgements and credits: Thank you - *Orin Zebest*

About the author

Deanna Keahey is the founder of Winning the Timeshare Game, and author of the associated series of timeshare books. She also writes about timeshare tips and news on her blog, _Winning the Timeshare Game_.

Her publication credits include:

* _Winning the Timeshare Game: Buying the Bargains_
* _Consumer Awareness Guide to Buying a Timeshare_
* _Timeshare Owners' Guide to Winning the Timeshare Game_
* Winning the Timeshare Game website and blog at _TimeshareGame.com_

Deanna has loved travel and adventure her whole life. She is a veteran of the travel industry, and for 7 years, ran an international tour company that operated trips in the US, Canada, Caribbean, Central and South America, and Europe.

Her timeshare experiences began with one rather painful (but funny in hindsight) timeshare presentation years ago in Mexico. Since that time, she's enjoyed many fabulous timeshare vacations. She enjoys learning the tricks of how to maximize timeshare use and value, and sharing those techniques with her readers. She hopes that everyone can get as much enjoyment out of timeshares as she does.

Made in the USA
San Bernardino, CA
19 July 2015